Seeing Venice

An Eye in Love

Seeing Venice

An Eye in Love

An Inner Travelogue with 94 Drawings by

FREDERICK FRANCK

DESIGNED BY MARTIN MOSKOF

CODHILL PRESS • NEW PALTZ • NEW YORK

Library of Congress Cataloging-in-Publication Data

Franck, Frederick, 1909-
    Seeing Venice : an eye in love : an inner travelogue with 94 drawings by Frederick Franck
        p. cm.
    ISBN 1-930337-04-3 (alk. paper)
    1. Venice (Italy)--Description and travel. 2. Franck, Frederick,
1909---Journeys--Italy--Venice. I. Title.

DG674.2 .F737 2002
914.5'310493--dc21

                                                        2002020810

Dedicated to the wonderful work of the "Save Venice Committee"

Table of Contents

1 ❧ *The Overture*

There are one thousand and one books on Venice, from the deluxe coffee-table photo-rhapsodies via the highbrow cultural and historic tomes to the lowbrow little guides for the one-day sightseer armed with camera and camcorder.

This book, however, is dedicated to those whose senses are not yet numbed, whose eye is not dulled by saturation with constant electronic imagery; to anyone in whom the artist-within survived all conditioning, and hence first-hand seeing still takes precedence over looking-at, un-addicted to purblind clicking of shutters.

In this book drawings and words are not separate categories, but form a single process: Venice is so much more than canals, bridges, gondolas. It is an unbroken sequence of ever-changing moods, festive, frivolous, elegiac and melancholy, forever foreign yet totally intimate. I retrieve here, unscathed, the visions of my Dutch childhood in the vastness of the Lagoon where round-nosed barges are still plying, swift sailboats and every kind of craft cleave the grisaille opalescences of cumulus, the diaphanous veils of vapor.

I did not "design" this book. It grew out of this process, quite riddlesome as it is. For it is a mystery, this image-making passion in which a surplus of wonder, of awe, seems to activate the hand to leave tracings on paper when the light strikes the fleeting forms of water, cloud, palazzo, human face, to fuse in lines and dots and words into a single living fabric, trusting that somehow a kindred eye may resuscitate these traces of pure experiencing in which the "Ten thousand Things and I reveal themselves as being of one root," as an ancient Chinese put it.

The process did not start at once on my first visit to Venice. I was over-whelmed by it. Venice became at once a fascinating object, while I remained the subject. Quite soon, however, subject and object fused, no longer separated from one another, when I started to draw that pillared, domed, scrolled, waterlogged dreamland. Venice started to project itself on my paper in lines, dots and words, this one city on earth protected by God and/or a lagoon from invasion by car, bus and truck, so that the only way to get around – apart from brief runs on the decks of vaporettos – is on foot.

I no longer looked-at Venice, I saw it, and so before I knew I was part of this city, felt at home, hence resisted buying a map. I could not admit I needed one. It took even longer before I bought a little guide book and skipped through the biography of the Most Serene Republic to discover that I had already read her history while drawing the stones, the carved lintels, capitals, columns and arches, while criscrossing Venice day after day, just following my nose, walking with eyes wide open, sketchbook at the ready.

I said walking: one cannot afford to trudge, for too much escapes the eye unless the head is kept mobile on its admirably designed swivel bracket. It has to shift constantly from marble pavement to wisps of cloud over the Piazzetta, from wisps of girls to formidable matrons, from deep black water to pillared facades, from tourists to gondolas, to all those stone tablets, set overhead in old walls: noble family crests, cherubs singing, angels winging, saints blessing, fabled animals, imaginary monsters. There must be a thousand winged lions on these tablets – they growl, smile, weep dejectedly – and numberless Madonnas who nurse their Babes, lift them for all to see, rock them, lifeless, on their knees in Pietas. One of these Holy Virgins

– she spans the Calle del Paradiso – spreads the cloak of her mercy over generations of us, ephemerals, who pass underneath.

"No architect should be allowed to practice his trade," says Professor Garrett Hardin of Santa Barbara, "until he has lived a year in Venice and knows what a city is, built to human scale." Not only is Venice built to human scale, it is the last surviving human city, the last habitat remaining on our planet still fully human in its patterns of hubris and humility, of life. Constantly astonished is one here by what should not be astonishing at all, except to us, so used, so conditioned to accept the machine's priority over all living flesh, to heed stop/go traffic lights, being demoted to the rank of pedestrian – that is, shorn of human rights until once again behind the wheel. Here, at last, the category pedestrian does not apply, for everyone still walks, or at most stands, once in a while compressed between fellow bipeds on the quavering deck of a vaporetto.

Venice is an immense and living indoor and outdoor studio. I can sit down to draw in peace on any bench, any stoop or folding stool, on any *campo* – as the squares are called here – in the middle of any street, whether narrow *calle* or wider *salizada* or dead-end *corte*. No one interrupts me or assaults me, no mugger robs me.

Submerged in this Venetian life, my seeing/drawing of Venice is both more and less than a declaration of love for the Serenissima, who has been loved by so many. Most of her lovers were writers. Goethe, Byron, Shelley, Ruskin shared in her favors, and batallions of lesser men of letters – of word – have reported all about her irresistible charms, her flawed and glorious past, so that not a shred of information needs to be added, and should any "information" sneak in to what follows, it might be considered as an adhesive to tie a few drawings together, both as witness and incentive to pure experience, an eye in love.

I return to Venice only when the Technicolor prettiness of summer has faded, the city has shed her garish summer dress. Venice only gives herself unreservedly on the sun-flecked foggy days of fall and early spring, and in the dead of winter, with hoarfrost on the tangled little wildernesses behind cracked garden walls. It is not comfortable to draw her then, with running nose and ice-cold fingers, but the light, a translucent grisaille enlivened with a moist pale gold sun, weaves the city and its shifting patterns of past and present in a warp and woof of scintillation and dimness in which the eye becomes fully identified with the water, the flights of pearl-grey pigeons, the timeless choreography of lovers. Old men in overcoats sit on benches, breathing in the sea air saturated with pollutants from the smoke stacks of Mestre and Marghera across the bay; discrete pollutants, just strong enough to gnaw away the noses and nipples of bronze and marble goddesses.

How still the city is in this greyness, where starlings can still be heard chirping, canaries mix their *bel canto* with the voices of children and cooing mammas. Far away, men are arguing in a twitter not noisier, yet not less noisy than a tree full of sparrows: choruses of life-sounds they are, in a timeless silence only made audible by the deep-throated throb of vaporettos.

It may seem that all those tourists flock to Venice for its Grand Canal, its *musea* and its gondolas. At one time this may indeed have been so, but now, whether they know it or not, they flee into this bosom of humanness from the chill boredom of their shopping plazas, their miracle miles, the dead and deadly souls of their graceless, frenzied cities.

An old man sits on a stoop, reading his paper, stops to shout his comments to a friend in a third-floor window across the yard-wide street. Stiffly he gets up, ambles home to his wife's pasta, still scanning the sports page. Lovers in their teens allow him to pass, push themselves – and each other – against the wall with mock courtesy.

This too is a symbol of Venice, perhaps more apt than the Winged Lion, for this is the city for humans, not lions or angels. These Venetians are neither. They are not exempt from Original Sin, these survivors from all the follies of history. They did not build their city in the sea for the lovely view, the clean air: they fled here for their lives, fifteen hundred years ago, before the waves of Visigoths and Huns and Ostragoths and all the other Nazis of their age, who burned their towns, raped their wives and daughters, put their babies to the sword. They fled from their war-cursed mainland, these early boat people, and built hovels wherever a high and dry spot could be found on the sandflats and mudbanks. They became fishermen and shipwrights and sailors, then learned to navigate and ventured further and further a-sea, until they traded all over the Orient. They became prosperous, then well-to-do, then rich, powerful, formidable, so that for a while they ruled the waves. The cleverest, the most ruthless among them became the Morgans and Rockefellers of their day, built themselves gigantic mansions – as all the old rich and all the new upstarts have always built maximal

mansions, massive tombs. They rented out their fleets to those fanatic block-heads, the Crusaders, those proto-tourists who, if one knew how to handle and to flatter tourists – in the Crusader's case with Te Deums, plain chant and plenty of Holy Water of which there was a lagoon-full – yielded handsome profits with which to build grander palaces and *campaniles* and churches to the greater glory of oneself and God, and this entire maze of living, teeming alleys in which to strut in glory for the admiring plebs during those few years one can still strut.

Venice managed to rule the waves for almost a thousand years, but even the great Ascension Day Ceremony, when the Doge was rowed in the golden Buccintoro, the state barge, to the Adriatic for his yearly renewed marriage to the sea, did not help. He flung a golden ring into the waves and declared, "I marry Thee, Oh Sea!" vowing eternal dominion over it, but seemingly, by Providence's decree, all the ruling of waves is strictly provisional.

And so Venice rose, and so it fell, until at last Napoleon could humiliate it, Austrian emperors conquer it, and finally the pre-paid tours invade it to be plundered in their turn.

It is this history that has made Venetians so resilient, charming, crafty and tough a breed as any on this planet. The only invasion it was spared, that by the motorcar, however, has preserved its humanness intact, protected it from becoming what the rest of us humans became: hybrids between mammal and appliance.

Having had to endear themselves to so many masters, Venetians also became superb actors and made Venice into their stage-set. Such born troupers they are, that they built their streets as stage-sets and backdrops for both their tragic and comic scenes, their heroic and villianous *tableaux vivants,* with hundreds of balconies from which one might blow kisses and throw red roses at serenaders below or with sweeping gestures harangue a cheering mob, balconies from which *en famille* to view pageants and processions, on which to dry the laundry, balconies from which, in adverse times, to be strung up to dangle in the sea breeze.

The street lighting of Venice either imitates stage lighting, or perhaps the latter was copied from Venetian ways of illuminating squares and thoroughfares for optimum dramatic effect. Their *campi* too were designed for histrionics, preferably Grand Opera, and Goldoni's *Commedia dell'Arte. Carmen* belongs on the Campo Bandieri e Moro, Gounod's *Faust* against the baroque facade of San Moise, *The Magic Flute* should be staged for a full house in the courtyard of the intimately feudal Palazzo Pisani, and all of Wagner – preferably in maximally heavy fog – against the facade of the Arsenale with all those eroded stone heroes, victories and lions.

Only the Campo Santa Margharita is unavailable, for here the human comic opera is booked up without intermission from dawn to midnight, seven days a week. Against a backdrop of fruit stalls, crates of calamari and scampi and displays of lovely pink nylon bikinis, the city's most mature minds gather to debate and steer the affairs of the world. Neither snow nor heavy fog deflects this self-appointed Council from its fateful responsibilities. Only during cloud-bursts – so as not to interrupt – the sages of the Campo take temporary shelter in the Bar dell'Sport.

2 ❧ *Axis Mundi*

It is generally assumed around the Campo Santa Margharita that the Axis Mundi surfaces here, roughly thirty feet northwest of the Trattoria Antico Capon, justly renowned for its Pizza alla Gorgonzola con Noci. According to the people of the nearby Campo San Barnaba this is not only superstitious, but a vicious propaganda ploy: They all agree that the pivot around which the world turns surfaces to the left of their well-head, as observed from the Bar dei Artisti. This, in turn, is ridiculed by loyal patriots of the Campo Bartelomei, the Campo San Giacomo and especially by the passionate chauvinists of the Castello. Who is right?

It is safe, however, to state that the world's Axis runs somewhere through this last of human cities, which happens also to be the last European one, as it will strike even the most superficial observer arriving from places like Brooklyn, Tokyo, even Hong Kong. In vain will he search for the Hilton of his hometown, for its Sheraton, Dunkin' Donuts, MacDonalds. In short, the European roots are still intact and unadulterated.

3 ❧ Venice – A Stage-Set

One evening – dusk was falling – I reached the Piazza when a martial extravaganza was about to start. A crowd had already gathered in front of Leopardi's three towering flagpoles that long ago replaced the last three trees that had graced the vast square. The tops of the poles and the flags that hung limp from them were barely discernible in the acrid fog that hurt one's eyes and made the facade of the San Marco their ghostly backdrop. It was too dark to draw.

A short ladder was leaning against each of the flagpoles, and at their foot stood two sailors at attention, one in the usual sailor's cap, the other with a brass helmet that covered half of his baby face. Two policemen stood trampling on cold feet. For a long time nothing happened. A Japanese tourist squatted, shot a flash. As I started to walk away I heard a barked command and, turning on my heels I saw a group of sailors, submachine guns under their arms, march out of the fog. They came to a stop at the ladders and froze at attention. Their commander, rigid as a statue, had his saber raised in front of his nose. Still nothing happened, but I noticed only now that at the foot of each of the masts a wooden box was standing. The officer cleared his throat, gave a hoarse shout, and instantly the three helmeted ones climbed to the top of their ladders, eight feet above sea level, while the ones in sailor's caps stood frozen in martial salute. The scene remained a motionless tableau for what seemed an eternity, but then the officer yelled again, and the men on the ladders started to loosen the flag ropes fastened there. The platoon presented its automatic weapons.

The unknotting proved less simple than expected. The sailor on the right was in trouble. He bobbed his head sadly, spread his hands, but his commanding officer ignored him. In the end, however, slowly, solemnly, the three flags came down in little spurts. They were unhooked and ceremoniously laid to rest, each one in its own box. The three elect now descended and with self-satisfied grimaces saluted once more. The flags were then quickly, almost contemptuously, stuffed deeper into their boxes and the lids secured. The officer swung his sword in a complex pattern, barked once more, and his platoon marched off across the Piazzetta into the fog. The policemen came to life at once, swinging arms, blowing whistles to signify that it was all over.

Yes, it was definitely over. The policemen disappeared into the bar at the corner of the Merceria; our shivering little audience slowly dispersed in the fog, leaving the Piazza dull and curiously empty. A French saying kept turning around in my head in that chill milky darkness: *"Nous sommes tous plus ou moins fou...."* We are all more or less crazy.

In a narrow street of the Castello section with its smelly tenements I saw in the distance a bright red light. It indicated nothing more licentious than a large pothole. But behind it, the shadow of San Francesco della Vigna rose into the gloom, the huge Franciscan church Palladio built on the spot where Saint Mark is said to have spent a night. A squat, bearded monk, all too medieval in his high fur cap and baggy habit, came shuffling out of a side door and left it ajar. I found myself in an

immense black cave, but deep in that nocturnal immensity shone a faint glimmer of light. Staggering over the uneven tombstones I reached it at last: It was the door of the tabernacle and it stood open. Inside, the

blackness seemed even more intense than the inkiness that surrounded it. I stood there, and an awe tinged with horror gripped me, made me want to flee and at the same time to kneel down. I saw forms loom up, flicker-

ing, fluid forms: the officer swinging his sword, the young sailors and the crowd, the bearded monk, this whole city, but also myself standing there, and my old house on the Wawayanda Creek in America. I saw my father, my grandmother, my son, the women I have loved, all I have loved, all of us fleeting condensations of this No-Thingness, sucked back into this Void the moment when, uncondensed, we fall asunder, we mirages of living here-ness...at once reality and illusion, Venice and you and I, this whole beloved world, this little planet, timeless fata morgana in the rush of time.

Venice, from this moment on, became more than the living city "built to human scale." It became a metaphor for our little planet, a pulsing metaphor for what threatens to become uncondensed the moment constellations of stars and tides — or just our own unfathomable follies — unleash the cosmic storm, the final conflagrations and inundations in which our city of man will flounder and all the greed and folly and cruelty of our predatory race with it. All the delusions of history will have become no-memories in no-mind. But also the greatness of that race will be lost as if it had never triumphed over all its baseness: the Christ in Glory of Vézelay who whispers "I and the Structure of Reality are not-two," the great Vairocana Buddha of Nara who proclaims that the Great Wisdom is the Great Compassion, and all the artists who have stated it in their own manner, in the Art of the Fugue and the bronzes of San Zeno, in Goya's "Disasters of War" and the smiling angel of the Cathedral at Reims, in Beethoven's last Quartets and Rembrandt's self-portraits and in the works of so many lesser ones who in the eye of God are no less, for all have testified to the divine spark of being Human.

And yet, is Venice the metaphor for our destiny? Or could it be the other way around? Could we be the metaphor for this sinking city with its emblem — the Winged Cat — on every pillar, street corner, souvenir mug, this indomitable noble Cat with two wings and nine lives, always fully alive to this present life, hoping and trusting that it is not yet the ninth, at most the eighth, perhaps only the seventh?

For this last of human cities, however threatened, is also living proof of an unquenchable vitality, a joie de vivre in the face of all threats of destruction and death, a sign of the affirmation of life in the face of the heart of darkness, the darkness that is heartless. Who will sink first? Venice? We?

4 ❧ Venetian Faces

At noon around the Pescheria, the fish market, and on the Campo Bartelomei, at the foot of Goldoni's charming statue in late afternoon, I draw the face of Venice, the Venetian face, absorbing it in bars, intoxicated by too much espresso, vino bianco and gallons of aqua minerale. The Venetian face can of course be contemplated on any campo, corte, in calle and salizada, but no observation post can compare with the bars: always stocked with the most authentically Venetian physiognomies. Not of course the famous Harry's Bar, where only the waiters are locals, and all the guests wear their German, English and American masks.

The little bars are my territory, although they are almost clubs, as exclusive as they are undistinguished, and where one penetrates with great diffidence, relieved at not being asked to leave at once.

There is such a club on the Campo San Agostin, but hard to find, for it is nameless, only marked by a rusty "Birra Wohrer" sign so dimmed by time and elements that it may be overlooked easily. Here on any afternoon, under a thick cloud of smoke, float the faces of the entire over-fifty male cast of the stage-set called parocchia San Stin. They play cards, and to them – at least full members of the club – the intruder is nonexistent, hence invisible. Associate members, somewhat below fifty, can be recognized by a furtive glance over their cards when the stranger enters; then they too deny his existence as required by the rules of etiquette. They push their hats back on their heads, throw down their aces on the varnished oak tables with yells of triumph or loud groans of frustration at divine injustice. Tilting their chairs backward, they spit theatrically on the sanded floor, as did their fathers and grandfathers on every afternoon since the late nineteenth century, and shout "Uno Prosecco!" "Uno Soave!" to the pasty-faced padrone, who was once a promising seminarian, but found his true vocation just before ordination, circa 1935.

By courtesy of the member's exquisite xenophobia, I am so thoroughly invisible that, should I strip naked and hang from the ceiling, they would look through me as if I were a wraith, yelling: "Uno Prosecco, Padrone!"

Another exceptionally fascinating panopticum, in the Calle Lungha Santa Maria Formosa, becomes lively around six when three generations find it irreplaceable for a well-deserved vino bianco after the day's troubles. It is drawn from huge canisters of yellow plastic, delicately camouflaged in traditional osier basketwork that fits the brown-black patina of the once white ceiling. Here local specimen swim in slow motion through the acrid smoke, come to rest at the counter, drink, spit, cough and kid around as if life were forever, yet all too short not to flirt with the bar maids carefully selected for their good legs, bovine grins and animal energy. This too is a club, far too exclusive to notice the old fool with his goatee who sits there scribbling in a sketchbook. They do see him, of course, for little escapes the Venetian eye that has seen everything under the metaphorical sun. But in the process it has become quite selective and does not differentiate between foreigners and their follies. Foreigners are customers, hence are welcome to be as foolish as they wish. This status of non-person fits me perfectly, allows me to scribble down this bouquet of faces, of genes of great variety, conditioned by Venetian history.

The faces one spots classify at once as British, French or Yank, and are faces programmed to the point where they become culture-specific variations on the human theme. They are not characterized so much by length or shape of nose or the color of hair and eyes, as by those conditioned mini-contractions of the muscles of neck and chin and around eyes, nose and lips, programmed from generation to generation. Amsterdam, Edinburgh and Boston produce their particular masks, destined to become more caricatured with age – could they be the masks of Original Sin? – as comic-opera Brit, Kraut, Jew, Yank....

The Venetian face is a cartoon of a much greater complexity, enriched as it is by infusions of Austrian, Spanish, Turkish, Greek and Balkan strains. How lithe and lively those little muscles play around nose and eyes and lips! How easily, how convincingly the Venetian face can smile the instant the footlights are switched on, to turn at once, offstage, to that creaturely, animal sadness, which at any moment is ready to turn again, instantly, charmingly, subserviently, sentimentally Venetian. This creaturely sadness must be carefully distinguished from the sob sister pose, or the tragedian's posturing that is part of the repertory, hence available at once whenever the stage directions prescribe it. The frown of patrician dignity à la Titian and especially the devout mien which, regardless of creed or its absence, must be switched on whenever circumstances demand it. The stage directions are highly detailed and explicit for all occasions. They are not in glaring contrast with those in Rome or Bologna, but they are at once distinguishable to the connoisseur.

Venetians seem to have acquired the rare capacity to draw a few useful conclusions from the myth called history, as well they might: Their own past of plundering and being plundered, raping and being raped, killing and being killed, made them end up in the tourist business. Meanwhile, they became hesitant about taking up the sword and perishing by it, preferring to find a more peaceful solution to conflict: compromises, deals, arrangements. This may account for the blissful sense of security the Most Serene Republic offers. You know where you are; you can trust the warmth, the cunning, the sentimentality and the humor, always keeping in mind that the stiletto is up the sleeve as a last resort, but that it is a metaphorical stiletto, wielded without letting blood flow. It is therefore naïve to complain about the absence of what we Northerners praise so highly as "principle," "commitment," and "decency" – that cruel decency, as cold as a filet of sole in a congealed sauce Mornay.

The "Bar all Orologgio" on the Campo Santa Maria Formosa is anything but clublike. Expatriates from far away dependencies of the Veneto, from Burano across the lagoon and even from San Erasmo, are not discriminated against; aliens from Verona, Hokkaido and Paterson, New Jersey, whose feet are killing them, are welcome to recover at one of the six tables, to be revived by an espresso, for which they will be charged four times the price of one if sipped standing at the counter. The man with the sketchbook loses his automatic invisibility here and has to fall back on his Vatican technique, learned empirically while drawing the Second Vatican Council in St. Peter's, to ward off nosey little cardinals shuffling all too close with ingratiating ecclesiastical smiles. This technique – quasi infallible – consists of throwing quick, angry glances over one's glasses, frowning ominously, while abruptly clamping drawing pad against one's chest. How else to draw the weekly kaffeeklatsch of the mature matrons in their fancy hats, distinguished mink-died rabbit coats over gallons of bust?

At the elegant historical Caffe Florian on the Piazza San Marco, none of these techniques will work. In its dainty drawing rooms of purple damask, golden lacquer, painted panels of odalisques of Arabian-Night fantasies, I hide my sketchbook demurely on my knee under the little marble table. The waiters are great Venetian actors, specialized in expressing such haughty insolence that the most impudent tourist, cowed and hushed, eats his brioche bashfully, handles the little porcelain cup with pinky refinedly stretched, for one is not allowed to forget, be it for a moment, that one's buttocks are supported by a chair that once may have carried the much more exalted ones of Lord Byron, Goethe, and, not to mention, of course, those of George Sand.

Did I really hear one of the two mature ladies, plucked eyebrows raised, gesturing so elegantly in the Chinese salon over there, the one in the large hat with tea roses, a marchesa, tell the contessa in the mauve turban, how as a little girl she rode on Nietzsche's knee, pulled Rainer Maria Rilke's goatee?

The Caffe Quadri across the Piazza, although almost as ancient as the Florian, has undergone such crude face lifts that all traces of distinction were lost, and even Richard Wagner, who once shook hands here with the little orchestra's Maestro after he had played *Lohengrin* in his honor, would fail to recognize the establishment, no longer part of the stage-set called Venice. Moreover, the orchestra's repertoire has recently been brought up to date all the way up to "Tea for Two." *Sic transit gloria mundi!*

5 ❧ *Concerto*

On a wall I saw a rain-soaked little yellow poster announcing a concert by a string quartet from Padua. Ah! A Brahms Quartet and Mozart's "The Hunt!" I jotted down the name of the palazzo where it would start at five, "by invitation only." Why the poster then? A Venetian riddle. I charged Signor Mario, part owner, reception clerk and breakfast waiter of my hotel, with the diplomatic mission of having me invited. Signor Mario, lanky with his solicitous little mask of wrinkled skin, started his career as busboy at the Danieli and the Gritti Palace in the bad old days when Benito played host there to Adolf. A lifetime in the hotel trade has taught him the graciousness that gives the modest Hotel Basilea its stamp of class.

"Avec plaisir, Monsieur le Professeur!" he smiled, for that is the title he conferred on me. It is a public relations ploy by which he converts, for the benefit of my fellow guests, my hardly prestigious wardrobe, my goatee, pipe and steel glasses into a social asset. He spoke rapidly and mellifluously into the receiver, bowed courteously at the words "contessa" and "professore" that he used with extraordinary frequency, and so I was made more than welcome. For similar emergencies I pack my only tie, a Tartan bow on a clip purchased in Edinburgh circa 1937 – the Tartan of the McLeans of Fife, I seem to remember – which has added significantly to my appearance during the decades, whenever a formal touch was required.

At the top of the scala mobile, the gala staircase of the palazzo, once strictly reserved for noblemen and their ladies, the quartetto was warming up. Waves of Brahms were braided with Presto trills of Mozart of the violin, and Adagio moans of the cello. The first violin, paunchy, pasty and sallow, strolled through the lofty hall rehearsing a vibrato. The cellist had a Pulchinella nose, the stooped viola player a much-too-long face in which the eyebrows rose to dazzling heights at every high note, to drop down to a pained frown at the lower ones, his thin mouth a-tremble like a guppy's.

In the drawing room twelve of us sat waiting on high backed Renaissance chairs. The bronze cardinal stared angrily from the marble rococo mantle, presumably our hostess' forebear, and was also hanging, in oil, framed in golden curlicues on the purple damask. Here he wore an expression of at once superhuman distinction combined with mildest benevolence, raising his slim hand with the great emerald ring in blessing over us, elect little remnant.

It was almost six when the warming up stopped, and the quartetto traipsed into the drawing room, sat down, and, after a final flurry of tuning, the first violin, with a tense little grimace to his colleagues, raised his bow. At once Brahms started to sing his grave ecstasies. I had my drawing pad on my knees, for I listen with my eyes, and with my hands as well as my ears. I saw the guppy mouth become a determined straight line, the Pulchinella became noble, the pasty violinist princely Roman.

Here they were, four grown men, after dozens of rehearsals, playing Brahms for our invited dozen, forgetting all, becoming all music, and I, listening with every fiber, was drawing them, their tenseness, as if everyone in that room were a merciless critic ready to jeer, to pan them contemptuously. Glorious poor devils they were, as are all of us artists, fools, dunces who pour body and soul into making the perfect picture in sound, in line, sure that the least imperfection is scandalously audible, visible to all. I, one of these fools, sat drawing them in anxiety of what would appear on the paper out of this mosaic of lines and dots that probably no other eye would ever see, or if by chance looked at, would at best be approved as a not-too-bad Polaroid shot made by hand.

During the heart rending slow movement the fool with the pencil had to stop. Eyes got too moist while listening and seeing these commonplace men becoming transfigured to noblest, most naked humanness. The pudgy hand holding the bow had become the most exquisite of elegance, the raising and dropping of the viola's eyebrows were full of secret meanings, the pasty face a majestic incarnation of human dignity. A deathless, timeless beauty is what I saw in this little group from Padua, foolishly playing their hearts out under the inane grimace of a cardinal long dead, while the worldly wise were making the money, the media and the missiles.

Blessed are the artists, those fools who can still hear and see and have found this childlike way to thank God for these gifts of hearing and seeing, quite content not to conquer the world, nor to save it, merely to love it.

The handsome lady two chairs away with her white hair in a bun had glanced a few times in my direction. During the intermission she and her husband decided to look at what I had been doing.

"Lovely day today, isn't it?" he said with the Oxford inflection that made it clear on precisely what rung of the social ladder he wished to be perceived.

"Would one be allowed to see what you have painted?" she cooed.

"Ah, Madam, I wasn't really painting," I said, "I was simply drawing. Please do forgive me; I don't even look at what I have scribbled until the morning after, at the earliest."

"Oh, do excuse me," she said with a very sweet little smile.

"Wonderful place, isn't it?" her husband added by way of gracious retreat, "Just too frightful it's sinking, isn't it, two and a half inches a year, I'm told."

An irate female voice interrupted: "Venezia is not sinkink!"

She was sixty-ish, in a floppy moss-green felt hat, a heather tweed tailormade and those sensible walking shoes that recall Fortnum and Mason's on Piccadilly. The string of pearls on her pink cashmere sweater was trembling.

"Venezia is not sinkink at all! Who says she is sinkink? I have been to England and to New York and even there I have spoken to many, many people who know that Venezia is not sinkink at all! So why do you say...."

Our noble hostess had become a porcupine in Harris tweed.

"You must have misunderstood, Madam," I said in a sudden inspiration, while looking at the poor Anglo-Saxons' plight, undone by such Latin passion in so British a garb. "What we were saying, madam, was precisely the contrary, namely that our world is sinking, unfortunately quite fast, so fast that according to the Club of Rome for instance, it is already sunk, hopelessly so. Of course, once it is incontrovertibly sunk, only then, we said, may it be Venice's turn."

I could be proud of my diplomatic acumen, for the Contessa relented, gave a vague smile of forgiveness and switched the subject to Brahms.

"He is a wonderful man, all dark passion, dark, dark, brooding passion," she sighed as if Brahms had just sneaked out of her boudoir.

"Quite!" smiled my neighbors, immensely relieved, "Oh, yes, quite!" as the musicians raised their bows again and let Mozart's Allegretto rise above us mortals – a lark hovering – powder-blue sky, timeless morning of Spring!

Urban diplomacy notwithstanding: The bottom of the lagoon is sinking indeed, and Venice with it. The sea is rising due to the melting of the polar cap, for which our technology seems only partly to blame, but "progress" is beyond any doubt responsible for what the heavy industry of Mestre and Marghera have done. It was not enough to mix their corrosive fumes with the salty sea air, they also had to drill fresh water wells indiscriminately all over the bottom of the lagoon, which caused the lagoon bed to settle. This drilling has been stopped and some anti-pollution measures are now planned. Unfortunately, the Piazza San Marco, the lowest part of the city, has been affected most. To see it transformed into a lake will be an unbearable Memento Mori.

6 ❧ *Death in Venice and Elsewhere*

Together, arranged like choristers on both sides of their Grand Canal, the palazzi chant an operatic requiem, part Verdi, part Berlioz in its orchestration, with dark blasts of Dies Irae trumpets.

Looked at individually these palazzi, famous or less famous, are often gigantic architectural wisecracks: vulgar cubes of brick and mortar hiding behind showy facades, as if contrived for a Renaissance Expo, with that surfeit of Gothic windows, Byzantine curvatures, Moorish and Greek pilasters, Roman columns and porticos, that whole inventory of hybrid railings, filigree stonework, lacy fenestrations, scrolls, arabesques, flounces, fringes and friezes that are such a desperate delight to scribble down, to disentangle while drawing.

But requiems they are, obituaries all effaced except for the great mercantile and noble names that still label them: Vendramin, Pesaro, Grimani, Mocenigo, Grassi. They stand contemplating their quavering reflections in the darkened mirror of the Canal, each one a phony hymn to the glory of bank accounts and bags of gold, each one a dirge for the rise and fall of prodigious fortunes. Each one too a monument to the folly of the mortals who built for themselves these marble-encrusted, all too ephemeral encampments. Impressive they are and functional, for their function was to impress, to overwhelm others with envy. How fortunate not to have seen this miracle mile of Renaissance ostentation when it was still new in its splashing polychromed and gold-leafed splendor, before the tens of thousands of pylons – the Dalmatian forests were decimated to support these conceits built on mud – had rotted away enough to let this proud magnificence sag wonderfully out of kilter, before sea salt and wind, plus half a century of industrial pollution, had smoothed all edges, dulled all panache. Even more fortunately, Bauhaus had not yet been invented to produce a soulless slum of brick cubes and concrete dice along these canals.

Erosion and those deposits of soot, salt, sulfur and sheer muck that, combined, we call patina, have at last mellowed and mollified all the bombast and pomposity, converted this entire rodomontade into a wondrous poem of never-intended textures, rare blends and interfusions of hues, of opaque and translucent opalescences, of moss-green and bottle-green shimmerings, degraded jade greens and Braque green effulgences, ochres, bisters, washed-out grays and quenched El Greco crimsons, as in a noble dirge on the transience of things and beings, of all their acts, of all their thoughts. Who has no eye for this, let him go shopping or feeding the Piazza pigeons.... But also on the Piazza one cannot evade this transience, this "death in Venice," that is not so unlike death elsewhere.

I saw the pigeon almost pressing itself against the wall of the Basilica, just beneath those red porphyry Tetrarchs, pilfered from Constantinople. Four Roman emperors, some say. According to others four Saracens turned to stone – they must have been *petite* Saracens – while robbing Saint Mark's treasure. The pigeon sat there. Her purple-green neck feathers, disheveled, stood on end. One ruffled wing was hanging down. Her left eye was closed, the right one stared wildly. A few times she tried to lift the slovenly wing, then let it drop again. She attempted a few steps, had to stop, then sat still again, her drooping head pulled back into the tangled, once glamorous collar. The right eye blinked a few times under a half-closed, gray eyelid. Slowly, in a terminal saraband, she turned around on failing legs, managed a full circle, tried to reverse the movement, shuddered faintly, collapsed on her side.

It was to be a day spent in meditation on life and death, for a few hours later I glimpsed Death again, near the Rialto where I was drawing a boy and a girl, brand-new lovers, standing on a bridge in the chilly drizzle to which they were oblivious. So fascinated were their eyes with one another's, so young a love it was –

no more than wonder, awe – that they could not yet touch each other, just looked and looked.

Then slowly, above the hump of the bridge, I saw a hat appear. It was an old-fashioned wide-brimmed straw hat, odd in the winter drizzle, with jet-black cherries on its brim. Then the face came into view: first dirty gray-yellow bangs, then a pair of dark cold eyes, the thin line of the mouth in a long and sallow face, and finally, a stiff old-maid's body in a black cloth coat. She did not see the lovers, for her pale eyes did not focus on anything at all, but the thin gray stockinged legs shuffled close to the lovers, her handbag brushed them lightly, for the boy who had his hand raised to touch the girl's face drew back as if stung. The girl stared in terror at the apparition.

On the Campo Bartelomeo Carlo Goldoni's charming statue ("Goldoni – good, gay, sunniest of souls...dear king of comedy, Thou that lovest Venice so...." Browning sang) stood smiling down on clusters of middle-aged men, arguing about nothing, but with ample gestures. Younger cocky ones were boasting of their adventures, mimed enormous leaps taken, giant fishes caught, magnificent bosoms and bottoms fondled. Coveys of giggling girls, arm in arm, were watching the handstands and cartwheels of the youths, applauding their feats, appraising them correctly as promising preludes of courtship.

In this town one's cuddled, cultivated misanthropy evaporates without a trace. The noise of human chatter simply becomes the music of life, the gloria in excelsis of a generation of sparrows in an oak, of young frogs in a green pond. But when I reached the high bridge across the Rio dei Santi Apostoli, there stood Death again among his Venetian props. A funeral barge lay waiting. The Requiem Mass had just ended, for a fat priest emerged from the Santi Apostoli in lace surplice to give urgent instructions to the pallbearers. Slowly the coffin was carried across the campo,

aboard the black launch with its carved tassels of roughly gilded wood, its golden lions dejectedly resting their heads on their front paws. Passersby made the sign of the cross, lifted their hats.

In the portal of the Church, a stout elderly woman with a black kerchief over her freshly set gray hair, stood wiping her red eyes. Friends and relatives filed past her, spoke a few words, kissed her on both cheeks. Wreaths and sprays of red carnations with gold, white and red ribbons were heaped on the deck. Grandchildren helped the old woman aboard. Behind the misted-over windows of the cabin the mourners sat chatting. The priest was still making gestures of blessing, when a man in uniform started the engine. It gave two snorts, then purred gently as the barge glided away, finding its way almost unaided by the wheel over the black water to San Michele, the Cimeterio.

What comes after death remains unanswered, but in the short-term perspective, death in Venice has something to be said for it. It is so comforting to be greeted respectfully a last time, with passers-by crossing themselves, to be properly absolved and prayed over even if it is mere habit, part of the programming; it is a civilized programming that symbolizes a certain reverence, be it post-factum, for human life.

It contrasted so with the adieux to Great Aunt Emmy, who just before I left New York had been rushed to St. Luke's to end her life connected to a battery of machines, two days earlier or later than if she had been left to die comfortably in her own bed, for she was eighty-nine.

When our little group of mourners arrived at the aseptic Westchester crematorium, we found that Emmy had been conveniently pre-cremated, ready for burial. After, as was tactfully requested, six hundred and forty-seven dollars and sixty-three cents were paid, a stout young man in black went to fetch Emmy, in a square card-

Off Campo Pantalon

board box that might have contained an alarm clock, and drove ahead of us to the spot where a neat square of Astroturf had been laid out with a square hole in it, a trifle larger than Emmy's box. All that remained to be done, he said, was to lower the box through that hole, courteously miming the procedure. He then sat on his haunches, nodding approval of the ritual, got up, smiled faintly, stepped into his car, and left.

Still, San Michele, the cemetery island with its massed black cypresses, behind the pink brick walls – subject of Bocklin's once famous, ultra-romantic painting "The Isle of the Dead" – has also become a bit businesslike recently, with its six-story-high blocks of efficiency apartments for the departed, neatly stacked one on top of the other like drawers in a jumbo commode. Each drawer has a name on it, a receptacle for flowers and usually a ceramic plaque with a photograph of its occupant, grinning pleasantly.

Nuns and monks of various orders still find peaceful lawns to sleep beneath, and for lay people not rich enough to afford white marble angels on their family vaults, black marble palm fronds are still available. Ezra Pound and Igor Stravinsky rest among ambassadors of the Austrian, Hungarian and Russian empires, Swedish counts, English lords and even a Queen of Greece in her unkempt, elegiac section of wild vegetation. For the others, unless a yearly fee is paid, eternal rest is compressed into ten years, after which they, or what remains of them, are unceremoniously dumped incognito into a communal pit, whatever confusion this may cause at the time of the Last Judgment. And yet, compared with Westchester....

There is a low windowsill at San Pantaleon, facing a charmingly dilapidated little palazzo on the other side of the Rio Foscari. I like to sit on it, after flicking away some fish bones of a cat's lunch. Vaporettos purr past, fast gray launches of the

Guardia di Finanza, with a moustached Garibaldi at the wheel, make great waves that drown the handsome Byzantine, horseshoe-shaped front entrance of my dream palazzo. Every now and then an ambulance launch with "Trasporto di Malati" in big white capitals on its side roars by, blue lights flashing, sirens yelling, throwing up a tidal wave that soaks my feet. It veers around the sharp curve, barely misses the abutment of the Ponte Santa Margherita, disappears in the direction of the Ospedale Civile, where the occupant is hauled up on his stretcher and wheeled inside, more dead than alive whatever his condition at the start of the race. A few black and gold funeral barges – an eminently practical arrangement – are always bobbing at this side entrance: San Michele is just around the corner.

Malicious foreigners may pretend to have seen armies of *staphylococcus aureus* thriving in the hospital's hallways, but I have witnessed someone leaving the Ospedale alive. She was lying on a luggage cart that, by means of a mattress, had been converted into an ad hoc stretcher. A man of fifty and a stout woman in a large hat wheeled her out of that side entrance. The form on the cart must have been female, for old women's shoes protruded from the heavy blanket that covered it, and it must have been alive, for it reacted when the woman in the hat bent over to shout at it. The man pushed the cart to the first bridge where he swung it around to make sure his passenger's head was more or less upright while the contraption was lifted over the bridge's hump by compassionate bystanders, who also helped at the second and the third bridge. The woman in the hat, meanwhile, fell behind, following lamely, blowing her nose, praying with her rosary: "and in the hour of our death, Amen."

7 ❧ *Lovers: An Aphrodisiac City*

On the rising and falling, creaking landing platform of the Accademia stop, lovers stand kissing goodbye, clinging to each other as if the farewell were forever. To see one's beloved off to subway or bus lacks all the poignancy of an embarkation across a gangplank, the waving adieu from bobbing landing to the unsteady craft sailing away into the mists. The anguish, the forebodings of these farewells, the anxious following of the vessel's wake, must be one of the active ingredients in the love potion called Venice, where sharing a minicruise aboard ship, even if it is no more than a vaporetto ride from station to Rialto, or a longer one, almost an hour, from Arsenale to Murano and back, may have the direst consequences. What on terra firma would be a casual kiss, easily escalates imperceptibly into an ecstatic water-borne affair, an unplanned euphoric elopement across the date-line to the point of no return.

But apart from cruises and farewells, there is something, until now, unaccounted for by science in the Venetian air, an ingredient apparently unrelated to atmospheric pressure and turbulence, to sea breezes, swamp-emanations and even astrological constellations, that acts as a powerful aphrodisiac.

Venetians themselves are relatively immune to it, so that they can go about their daily chores almost unaffected, although their long siestas are said to be less inactive than they might seem. Also, their women, from telephone operator to contessa, who are usually very well-apportioned ("Only dogs love bones," as a local proverb has it), seem puzzled and hurt if a male – any male – does not appear radically unsettled by their charms. The men, of course, cooperate to the best of their ability: their home training in macho has prepared them thoroughly for it. Strangers to the city, however, regardless of age, color or creed, are as a rule defenseless, overwhelmed by aphrodisiac turbulence. Behavior patterns change almost at once, and crucially. Archaic hunting and mating instincts assert themselves in limping old-age pensioners, purple-haired maiden ladies, and monks. Milquetoasts undergo hormonal muta-tions. Wherever the eye wanders, lovers are interlaced, from hardly hatched newborns to arthritic ancients, and all phases in between.

The phenomenon is curious. No virus has been isolated. Fluctuations in temperature cannot be blamed. The effect of sudden surges of humidity, however, cannot be ruled out.

8 ✣ *Rainwalk/Ghetto*

When rain and sleet hit, the Serenissima shows herself naked in the unbearable melancholy of her old age. It is the right instant to don raincoat and rubbers, to slosh through the downpour along the Canale Canareggio, then turn right through the dank passage tunneled under houses, the sottoporteggio, into the Ghetto, divided into the Old, the New and the Newest Ghetto, together one confined little universe of affliction, which no blue sky can enliven, no sunshine cheer.

Ever since 1560 the Jews of Venice were constrained to live here behind heavy gates locked each night and guarded by mercenaries whose wages they had to pay. They were so overtaxed, levied under any pretext, charged such a high lease for their isolation ward, that by 1735 the community had been milked dry, and the Inquisition had to declare it officially bankrupt. The Most Serene Republic itself was insolvent by this time, but still loathe to admit it.

The Jews may have been segregated in their ghetto, but they were not persecuted. In contrast to the practice of other "Christian" states, they were even protected by law from arbitrary torment, humiliation, mob violence and massacre. In the sixteenth century the ghetto actually prospered. Foreign visitors marveled at the distinction and beauty of Jewish places of worship – no less an architect than Longhena, builder of the Salute, built and refurbished the "Spanish" synagogue – and at the elegance of their women, "bedecked with jewels like countesses." Jews were bankers, sought after as physicians, wrote learned treatises on philosophy, traded in the Titians, Tintorettos and fine furniture which an impoverished nobility was forced to sell and foreign dignitaries were keen to acquire to add glamour to their mansions.

Architecturally the ghetto is an oddity. The houses on its campo – they had to be blind toward the city and face inward – lack all Venetian charm and ornamentation. An ever-expanding population made it necessary to place story upon story until the ghetto became an avant-garde experiment in the building of austere high-rises. The Winged Lion of Saint Mark may have torn more than its pound of flesh out of this ghetto community; it survived after its bankruptcy, until it was Napoleon's coup de grace to the Most Serene Republic that opened the heavy gates. By then the ghetto had become home to a majority of Venetian Jews, who remained faithful to it until the Nazis came, who, flouting all law, human and divine, massacred them all. The remaining synagogues are said to be worth visiting, but I have lacked the courage: the campo itself in its desolation is too unbearably haunted by the ghosts of thousands of men, old and young, women, boys, girls, hounded into freight barges, driven into cattle cars by uniformed anthropoids, who butchered them in those abattoirs for humans they invented and perfected.

The bridge crosses a canal, ironically named Rio della Misericordia, the Canal di Compassion, which leads to an almost equally bleak neighborhood of sagging, huddled houses and crumbling mansions on four long, thin islands separated by malodorous canals. A dismal hospital

of dark brick, and a pride of leprous, hunchbacked, arthritic palazzi stand contemplating the reflections of their faded glory in black water pockmarked by heavy bubbles of rain, singing their Miserere, telling tales of infinite woe.

Suddenly the living rain lashing my living face banishes all dejection, and at once, the gray melancholy shattered, wet brick, black water and charcoal-gray sky become symphonic. Across a little bridge, I bump into the pink brick church of San Alvise that has stood blushing here for the last six hundred years. The old house that flanks it could have been thrown there by Soutine's brush, so drunkenly out of whack it leans against Alvise's side. The Tiepolos inside the church are hidden behind plastic sheets. To protect them? To protect us? Has perhaps some keen cleric come to suspect the great virtuoso of satirizing sacrosanct subject matter? A reasonably good Catholic of the Venetian variety, Tiepolo, this Don Juan of painting, would not have dreamed of such mockery. He simply confused – and not so much more than did his brothers of the guild – religious expression with Grand Guignol. Tiepolo just was not born to paint icons, as Matthias Gruenewald was not made to decorate the ceilings of boudoirs and love nests with lusty, topless goddesses riding flying stallions. Perhaps Tiepolo was born to draw, do nothing but draw: his and Guercino's are the most alive, witty, incisive drawings before Pascin's or Felicien Rops.

The rain has changed to sleet meanwhile, and I retrace my steps, for I never set foot in this neighborhood without paying my respects to the three venerable Moors set in a wall on the Campo di Mori, just off the Fondamente della Senza. One of these thirteenth-century life-size Moors, the one on the corner of the quay, lost his nose centuries ago and, in a forerunner of plastic surgery, had it replaced by a disproportionate proboscis of cast iron that made him a figure of fun, Sior Antonio Roba,

still a Pulchinella figure in Venetian farce. The two other Moors gravely flank the entrance to the Palazzo Mastelli, built by a family of seafarers almost as prominent as Marco Polo's.

The facade of the Abbazia that stands at the very end of the quay overlooking the great empty harbor basin, the Sacca della Misericordia, is an overloaded orgy of eighteenth-century Baroque, by now pitted and eroded, but next to it in the blind wall – as if to make up for all this petrified hysteria – a chaste bas-relief, Byzantine and austere, of the Virgin, her hands lifted in *orante*. She is saying prayers for all that is born, must live, must die and vanish.

Do I hear high women's voices singing? Are there still nuns in the Abbey? It is all too easy to imagine things in this snowy stillness, this living silence now extinct in all cities but this one. The desolate vastness of the deserted harbor suddenly springs to life with galleons and frigates and oddly ornamented barges, with generations of sailors and condottieri with their wives, their dark-eyed concubines, their children. I see uncouth crusaders on the deck of Dandolos' flagship, bargaining with the stubborn, blind old doge, wrapped in wolf skins, on his gold throne. All these imprints in the ether become touchable in this silence, all the built-in filters fail. Present becomes past, past becomes present, all that is outside is perceived as inside. Once the filters fail, the ear hears far away footsteps on the flagstones as loud chords, the falling of the sleet in the water as a hissing whisper. The eye focuses with such intensity on these old quays that they abandon themselves without holding anything back, offer themselves naked with all they ever had, everything worth possessing, everything but silence.

I weave my complicated way through the alleys around the Sacca to see it from the opposite side. By the time I reach the Fondamente Nuovo the sleet has stopped. A thick mist now hides the Abazzia. The great mansion on the promontory is barely visible, floating vaguely, raggedly out of focus in the fog, impossible to draw of course. Still a door stands ajar, and the dirty hallway makes an instant studio.

The specter of a vaporetto glides close by, the shrieking of an ambulance, its steel-blue light flashing through the fog, streaks past. As I stand drawing from my stinking shelter, the mansion too dissolves and all is blotted out. Yet only now I notice the shadows of a thousand wings beating in the pea-soup fog. A speckled gull, majestic and evil, alights on the mooring buoy that almost touches the quay: three mighty logs, black and mossy, held together by a hoop of heavy steel.

"Where two or three are gathered in my name...."

The evil gull, at once, turns into the Dove.

I wade through the slush and refuse of the alleys that run from here to the Rialto, alleys of unspeakable squalor. I follow a man bent double under the heavy mattress he carries on his back. Then, looking up, in quick succession, my eye falls on stone tablets set in the walls of this infernal slum: one of an angel supporting a coat of arms, another tablet with such a shield held between the forepaws of a gentle lamb, a third one on which, surrounded by a wreath of laurels, a strong male arm crosses a slender female one. Leering stone heads protrude from a sheer brick wall.

Why am I standing here, old fool, drawing with stiff fingers in the cold fog? For whom? And on cheap paper that won't last thirty years.

Cheap paper or marble, thirty or fifty or five hundred years, does it matter? Where will all this be in thirty years, and you? And I? Why do I stand here? To catch the moment when all the filters fail...and the stones can start to tell their tales. Every one of these stones has been carried by men from elsewhere, for here was only sand and mud. Straight from the quarries of Istria, perhaps, or from Torcello when its harbor silted and it fell to ruin, or from overseas as did many of San Marco's stones. For each stone a ship owner imported to build his own palace, he had to contribute one for the Basilica. Each single one of these Venetian stones was quarried, hewn to shape, carved into lintels, heads, cherubs, caryatids, by human hands, and placed in the facades. All these stone heads that emerge from sheer walls, heads that sing, laugh, frown, tragically noble heads, like that of the stern young woman on the Zattere, some divinely smiling, as that of the girl who for centuries had mirrored herself in the Rio Munaghete, or those thirty-six heads in every possible mood on the virtually hidden side wall of the Ca Rezzonico, and finally at the base of the clock tower of Santa Maria Formosa that "monstrous face" that shocked Ruskin so, "that most foul" head, which he felt embodied "the evil spirit to which Venice was abandoned in her decline."

In our century of cruel evil, haunted by the "most foul" masks of Hitler, Stalin, Idi Amin among all those others, it looks quite tame, this head, perhaps a mascot against the evil eye.

9 ❧ *La Chiesa*

"No state has ever exercised a greater moral influence over its subjects, whether at home or abroad," wrote Jacob Burckhardt, who somewhat oddly adds: "Every Venetian away from home was a born spy for his government," and that "As a matter of course the Venetian cardinals in Rome sent home news of transactions of secret papal councils."

Such lofty honorability – by their own Venetian norms – has remained proverbial. Nevertheless, even today, violent crime is a rarity among the natives. Some believe this can be ascribed to centuries of fear of being sent by the Council of Ten – and without appeal – across the Bridge of Sighs to the dungeons where, after a brief consolation by a hooded monk, one might be quietly strangled or perhaps more formally executed on the Piazzetta. One doge set a radical example by having his own son strung up "as the common thief he was" when the scoundrel, skillfully leading an innocent maiden to the point where she allowed him anything his heart desired, took off with her string of pearls.

In case of regrettable miscarriages of justice, noblesse obliged the Council to make amends, as for the poor baker who was hanged long ago for a crime he had not committed and for whom the two lanterns on the side of the San Marco are still lit every night. Others hold that not only fear of the executioner kept Venetians in line, but at least as much dread of their patron Saint Mark's all-seeing eye, under the scrutiny of which every citizen lived from cradle to grave and well beyond, and kept them practicing good citizenship. On their perilous sea voyages Saint Mark's eye followed them, checked on their conduct, particularly on the fulfillment of their religious duties. Returned home safe and sound, the Saint's good will was at least as indispensable as to survive the next plague. Obviously, not even an apostle-emeritus could protect each and every Venetian at home and abroad personally, and it was therefore fortunate that he could count on an efficient team of aides like San Eustacchio, San Zaccharia, San Geremia, San Nicolo, San Stin, San Crisostomo, San Sta, San Sebastiano, two San Giacomos and two San Simeons, Piccolo and Grande, to mention just a few to whom elegant churches are dedicated.

Honoring the Holy Virgin herself, there are numberless oratories, sanctuaries, chapels, shrines, churches, statues, bas reliefs on facades, bridge abutments, sheer walls, street corners. Madonnas are perched on steeple tops, cupolas, garden walls, with or without wrought iron umbrellas to protect them against summer sun and winter squall. According to reliable statistics, the Virgins outnumber the Winged Lions although other trustworthy statistics prove the opposite. Among the doge's duties of office was the attendance at the annual feasts of all Saint Mark's assistants who had their share in every triumph of the Serenissima's fleets, armies, merchants and bankers.

The devotional mien that is part of every born Venetian's repertoire may well have developed as a protective maneuver against Saint Mark's unrelenting quality-control. To pull one's facial muscles into the proper grimace for ecclesiastical use, to look properly pious on occasions that require it – funerals, wakes, baptisms – to genuflect, to cross oneself when etiquette demands it, is instilled simultaneously with toilet training. These signs of piety carry no obligation, least of all that of believing in anything whatsoever. It is simply a conditioned reflex automatically activated when the moment demands it, orthodoxy, heterodoxy, even militant atheism notwithstanding.

Whether these sly traders, soldiers of fortune and sea captains were ever

very religious in the sense of "ultimate concern," to use Tillich's expression, no one will ever know. But it is certain that the role of organized religion in the Most Serene Republic was extremely covetous and manipulative. The Crusaders, for instance, were celebrated with the extravagant pomp and circumstance of Masses and Te Deums. State and Church lived together in close, yet antagonistic symbiosis, frequently at violent odds, as recorded in repeated interdicts and anathemas. The anticlerical strain in the Venetian character has always been strong. Richard Wagner, who loved Venice so dearly that in 1883 he died there in the Palazzo Vendramin – now a Casino – wrote that he saw "a procession of clerics cross the Piazza in their vestments, openly mocked by the people." On that same Piazza during the latest Carnevale, it struck me that among all costumed attractions the mock-bishop preceded by a little boy swinging a censer and followed by a three-year-old nun, as well as the purple cardinal dripping with smiling benevolence and accompanied by a simpering acolyte, both making signs of the cross and blessing the revelers, were the greatest sources of hilarity.

Church and State however have always seen eye to eye in an appetite all of Venice shares: that for ceremony and pageantry. It is still as strong as when Carpaccio recorded it in its archetypal form in his "The Miracle of the Cross" in the Accademia, a painting that at the same time sheds light on the devout mien, that mask of piety indispensable for such pageantry, still functional and useful in today's secular city. Its function is no longer political in a Venice as communist as Rome and Bologna, but still....

In this city with too few parks it is extremely hard to find a spot suitable for a declaration of love, and even less for the expression of it, which demands minimal privacy. Fortunately Venice's many churches are hardly overcrowded on weekdays; most are mercifully empty and have dark corners, like the one I fled to during a shower.

I saw them enter San Salvatore one by one, he in overalls, she in a short jacket of faux mink. Separately they genuflected, crossed themselves with holy water and, from opposite corners, proceeded, hands demurely clasped in front of abdomen, to the third side-chapel on the left, where they knelt side by side on the prie-dieu. Soon the hands unjoined, and touched, at which point – not being a voyeur – I started to draw the angels that flanked the altar. The custodian, who also had glanced in their direction, continued to dust the lectern on the Epistle side with great concentration. At twelve-thirty sharp he stopped, dragged his heavy shoes audibly to the vicinity of the love chapel.

"Hm!" he coughed. *"E dodici e mezzo! Vorrei chiudere, scusi!"*

The lovers disentangled, at once donning the devotional mask. The girl shook her hair, pulled down her jacket. Her lover, as a sign of gratitude, left a small donation for the poor, to be administered by the custodian. Then they walked to the door each in pious isolation, turned around and genuflected. She left first into the crowded campo. He stayed behind a few moments longer, lost in prayer, until the custodian rattled his keys.

Is it not written: Thou shalt love thy neighbor?

San Salvatore may have its uses during a rainstorm: Santa Maria dei Miracoli is a church for all seasons. It was built by a merchant, Ammadeo, who during the plague of 1480 vowed that should he and his loved ones be spared, a church would rise on the site of the little shrine where he prayed his Ave Maria daily on his way to the office. He kept his word and commissioned Pietro and Tullio Lombardi – who also fashioned that delightful little bon-boniere, the Palazzo Dario on the Grand Canal – to build the Miracoli, quite un-Venetian but pure Renaissance that still enchants the eye – perhaps even more than ever – for its white, green and russet marble encrustations have faded melodiously, and before its restoration its every angle had become dislocated, sagging delicately. Inside, Palestrina masses, recorded but very tender, waft – candlelight made audible – through the lacy fenestrations of the marble altar-screen.

Another sanctuary dedicated to Mary, almost its opposite, is Santa Maria del Giglio, also known as the Zobenigo, after the patrician family that erected it, less, one supposes, ad majorem Dei gloriam than to the glory of its own riches and power. Its seventeenth-century Venetian-Baroque facade is so heavy with sculpture that not an inch of space is left for the imagination, religious or otherwise, sacred or profane.

On a gusty morning I have stood in front of these prodigious fireworks of stone, trying to draw it, to come to terms with its surfeit of forms, trying to solve the riddle of this obsession with cornucopias of naked bodies, legs, arms, helmets, spears, banners, clarions, coats of arms, garlands of fruit and leaves, cherubs, fabled animals, this entire horror vacui that cannot leave a nook unstuffed with busy shapes.

The interior of the Zobenigo is arid in comparison, but a sign with a large arrow boasts of a Rubens in the Tesorio, a painting that only proves that even a Rubens, if he should be responsible for it, had his off days. But this treasure room contains a remarkable enough collection of reliquaries, elaborate confections of precious metal and stones that frame the osseous mementos of saints, both famous and obscure: for instance, a well-turned shinbone of a Saint Concordia and a tiny particle of Catherina of Siena, of whom one might as well adore the complete foot owned by San Zanipolo. A fastidious piece of gold-smithing frames a few of Saint Francis's hairs, an even more intricate one surrounds a thorn from the Crown of Thorns. On this cold day shivering tourists, finding little else to train their Nikon on, use the old fellow drawing these holy bones as a substitute target, for the tourist regards all of creation as a curio God created for this purpose alone: to be shot at. An adolescent couple glued together between a haughty silver saint of questionable rank and a splinter of John the Baptist is oblivious to the clicking of shutters in its celebration of the bliss of bones still covered by warm flesh. But I gave up when I felt a camera leaning on my shoulder for a close-up of my sketch pad.

I leave it to John Ruskin to speak of the San Marco:

"A multitude of pillars and white domes clustered into a long, low pyramid of colored light, a treasure heap it seems, partly of gold, partly of opal and mother-of-pearl, hollowed beneath into five great vaulted porches, ceiled with fair mosaics and beset with sculpture of alabaster clear as amber and delicate as ivory, until at last, as if in ecstasy

the crests of the arches break into a marble foam and toss themselves far into the blue sky...."

What I see is a vast sober reliquary, a sacred hollow in which one floats as in a dream, old-gold and muted purple. In flashes the eye catches fragments of the vast mosaics, bone-white and black visions imbedded in burnished gold, centers of satori: the Nicopeia Madonna, the Pala d'Oro, the mystic signs in jasper, porphyry, marble floors, pillars and capitals. The San Marco must be entered at dusk, when the crowds have left, the daylight paled and the Duomo becomes a riddle and the riddle has no solution, for what human hands built here is of sheer mystery, of infinite human latencies become manifest which the mind cannot encompass.

On the high Ponte della Stazione, three nuns, each one carrying a formless black briefcase, stood in the drizzle. The two older ones, as squat and formless as their bags, were arguing heatedly. The third one, much younger, was just waiting. First she stood staring at the traffic on the Grand Canal. Then I saw her turn her head to the station. A train had just arrived. Young couples, old couples, couples arm in arm, couples growling at each other, couples celebrating their Venice outing with shameless kisses under umbrellas.... She had turned around now, swinging her heavy briefcase to-and-fro, trampling in the gray rain, watching.

San Giacomo dall'Orio on its tree-shaded campo has none of the grandeur of the San Marco. It is of unaffected inwardness, untouched by the rising and falling of history's ebb and flow, as if it were standing somewhere on a mountain top, unreachable even by the high tides of tourism. It is not included in the "musts." Dark and taciturn, its entrances hard to find, no one corrupted it, made sanctuary into museum, no polyglot guides offer platitudes.

San Giacomo simply is not this, not that. It is. It still echoes sacred messages in a code that is lost, whispers meanings to be pondered, not articulated, wordless prayer. Its frescoes are homey, its polychromed Madonna rustically maternal. Could its secret be condensed in the twelfth-century Crucifix that hangs in a side chapel against the bare brick wall? Is it a crucifixion, or a resurrection, or both at once, this Christ of wood, without cross, who hangs there, this Christ who smiles with a smile from The Other Shore?

It is not the Buddha's smile of supernal wisdom, detached compassion. Yet it has all the wisdom and all the Compassion, but distilled through all the joys of body and spirit, all exaltation and all the terror, all the pain that flesh can endure. It participates in all the greatness and all the bottomlessly cruel, blind absurdities of our human species, which never sees what it looks at, hence never knows what it does, what it perpetrates. It is as if this fully Human Christ cries his "It is finished," and rising to Heaven, smiling, whispers: "It is not, oh no, it is not finished, it is not finished...."

The Christ of San Giacomo, the Nicopeia Madonna of San Marco: to this agnostic, this not-knower, are the harmonious poles, male and female, of this still human city, this Serenissima.

10 ❧ *Gondoli, Gondola*

For the one-day-two-night tourist, the prepaid Venice package is condensed into two snapshots. The first one, inevitably, is of one's partner smiling broadly, covered by a dozen filthy Piazza pigeons; the other, the beloved smiling – romantically now – in a gondola, reclining.

As soon as the weather permits, evening after evening, fleets of solidly bunched gondolas float down the dark Grand Canal into the Rio Foscari with baritones and accordions bellowing "O sole mio" and "Gondoli...gondola" for the benefit of ever new waves of Germans, Japanese, Nigerians and Midwesterners waving at their doubles hanging over the balustrades of bridges, shooting flashbulbs at one another.

I am envious of their blessed simplicity, but am constitutionally as bereft of the courage to join them in their rite, as I am unnerved by the idea of posing in Volendam costume on the Zuiderzee, as an Indian brave on a boardwalk, too snobbish even to stick my head through the hole in a two-dimensional samurai for the snapshot to be sent home from Mount Fuji.

Unsuited as I may be for the gondola ritual, I delight in drawing the elegance of these swift, gleaming black craft with the silvery ferro, the iron ornament on their bow that acts as a counterweight to the gondolier standing on the poop. Gondolas have been part of the Venetian scene in some form or other since the

flat-bottomed vipera was invented in the fourth or fifth century, a swift slender craft that could glide and curve on the often very shallow lagoon. In Carpaccio's "Miracle of the Holy Cross," in the Accademia Museum, they had already assumed their present form, be it without the metal ornamentation that became part of it in the eighteenth century and which besides being functional is symbolic: the ferro is an ornamented diagram of Venice itself. Its hatchet-shaped body is the stylized horned cap of the doge, the six short bars that extend to fore symbolize the six sestieri, or districts; the seventh longer one that extends aft, stands for the island of Giudecca. The swanlike neck extends down the length of the prow as a metal shaft, S-shaped to represent the Grand Canal itself. In Venice's heyday there were more than a thousand gondolas, adorned even with golden prows, competitive status symbols for the rich. Later in the sixteenth century this all-too-conspicuous consumption had to be curbed by law, and later, after a particularly lethal epidemic – or perhaps as a sign of mourning for the loss of the Peloponnesus – they had to be uniformly painted black.

The only gondola rides my snobism allows me to take are the short, utilitarian ones of the traghetto between Fishmarket and Ca d'Oro, or from San Gregorio near Santa Maria della Salute to the San Marco district. The fare for these unromantic ferry rides by shabby old craft is less than a dime, but the gondoliere is devoid of straw hat with red or green ribbons and there is no American Express baritone aboard to serenade the housewives with plastic bags full of escarole and cala-

mari, a poor chicken dangling head down in extremis, and perhaps a few old-age pensioners on canes, still agile enough to lower themselves stiffly into the bucking craft, but too short of breath for the climb across Rialto or Accademia bridge.

Gondolas that are sick or disabled undergo surgery on one of the little wharves just across from that forbidding repair shop for humans, the Ospedale Civile. There are dozens of these wharves, lining the backwaters around San Pietro di Castello; as in a living nineteenth-century copper engraving they form a jumble of masts and ropes and rickety cranes, with swarthy men hammering and welding and filing. The most remarkable one of these wharves, however, is the little one on the Rio Trovaso, as if sketched into the Venetian cityscape by Hokusai himself in a bout of nostalgia for Kyoto and Kamo river. Its sheds of weathered nut-brown planking are overshadowed by a gnarled old pine tree that could serve as the backdrop for a Noh play but that stretches its venerable limb over a wounded gondola lying on its belly across rough trestles, like a dying black swan.

11 ❧ *Santa Maria della Salute*

The feast of the Virgin Mary's Presentation in the Temple on November twenty-first is such an exceptional occasion that for this one day a temporary iron footbridge is laid across the Grand Canal. It leads directly from the San Marco precinct to the great Church of Santa Maria della Salute. It was a dreary, shivery Sunday; such a thick fog had settled over the city that all day long only the melancholy dirge of foghorns succeeded in piercing it, although some roses on the flower stall at Santa Maria del Giglio were of such deep red warmth that they glowed briefly through the grisaille at noon.

The sellers of votive candles at the iron bridge stood blowing on their fingers, but business was brisk, for a dense crowd streamed constantly toward the Salute; not tourists with cameras, but Venetians who had come from all six boroughs with their children to pay homage to the Virgin, in their Sunday best. In mid-afternoon, buildings, canals and boats vanished completely in impenetrable fog, and there was only this silent, joyous and ghostly procession of humans carrying candles and red roses across the spooky bridge.

Joining this timeless silent trudging, I felt myself dissolving in this crowd of living phantoms. A sense of evanescence penetrated one as deeply, as chillingly as the fog. I was aware that those behind me saw me reach the hump of the bridge to fade away in the vagueness, knowing they would be next. It was as if each moment was one's last, yet timeless, forever. Everyone, the one in front, the one behind, became oneself.

Once inside the Salute, Longhena's seventeenth-century masterpiece built to express the Venetian's gratitude for survival after a frightful plague, everything sprang sharply into focus again: The great octagon was filled with thousands of people, small as ants under the soaring height of this coldly brilliant, geometrical architecture of gray stone pillars dividing whitewashed walls. On the altar the Virgin stood splendidly enshrined in roses, in front of her in lace surplices on a high platform choristers stood chanting Maria-hymns.

Slowly, meekly, the thousands with their candles climbed the few steps from the immense octagonal ambulatory to the sanctuary. Here choir boys gathered the burning tapers, placed them in great iron chandeliers, left them to flicker for a few minutes until replaced by newly arrived ones. In the sacristy behind the altar glassy-eyed oldsters sat hunched in overcoats in the carved choir stalls. A prelate in black with purple piping – intelligent, ultra-Italian, aquiline of profile – stood at the exit, cordially patting, touching shoulders, shaking hands, measuring precisely the appropriate dosage and quality of smile and gesture.

Outside in the fog, past stalls of edibles, toys and souvenirs, the narrow quay to the Dogana was slippery, the water invisible. A large, dark phantom ship was making a hesitant full turn, bells ringing, horns roaring, search lights thrown back by walls of condensed vapor.

There are a litany of names of Mary: Santa Maria della Salute, Santa Maria del Giglio, Santa Maria Formosa, Santa Maria della Fava, della Miracoli, dell'Orto…. Even in the Basilica dedicated to Saint Mark it is the wonderful icon of the Nicopeia Madonna – which according to legend was painted by

Saint Luke and, according to history, stolen from Byzantium by Doge Dandolo's men – that is the central focus of devotion: a goddess of mercy, a Western Kwan Yin, I often thought.

In Kyoto, on the enormous, hundred-yard-long altar of the Sanjo-sangendo Temple, stands a gigantic statue of Kwan Yin or Kwannon, surrounded by a thousand life-size Kwannon images, each one representing thirty-three manifestations of divine mercy, making a total of thirty-three thousand embodiments of infinite compassion, a cascade of merciful grace. Actually Kwannon is the Bodhisattva, Avalokitesvara, but this does not affect the popular imagination that made this Enlightened One into a Kami, a god or goddess. The Japanese Kami however, are not analogous to a Greek god. Their Kami are rather divine Presences manifested, for instance in a sacred tree or spring, or in a great hero or poet. Enshrined in the *jinja*, its sanctuary, such a Kami becomes the protector of village or town, of a circumscribed place.

Does not the Virgin too carry innumerable topographical names? In my Dutch hometown she is the miraculous Star of the Sea; in Mexico the Madonna of Guadeloupe standing on her crescent moon; in Spain the black Madonna of Montserrat; the protectress of Poland is the Virgin of Czestochowa. The Virgins of Lourdes and Fatima have been healing presences, "full of grace," for untold faithful. The list of miraculous virgins is endless. Superstition? Perhaps, but less cruel than the new superstitions of progress, of gadgets, of technology as the way to happiness, of nationalism and all the political credos that demand human sacrifice in infinitely greater numbers than Aztec liturgies.

And are not these Venetian Madonnas the Kami of this circumscribed patch of earth?

A few years ago in the little Dutch village of Zegge, I entered the village church and saw the seventeenth-century peasantlike heavy-set Virgin, gold crowned and all dressed up in sky-blue velvet, bedecked with jewelry. Villagers came to kneel and pray: to pray to the goddess of their home ground, and suddenly I saw that whosoever failed to pay profound homage to such a Kami of Place, this Magna Mater, doomed himself to remain forever alien to the very ground he stood on.

Here in the Salute the vision came even clearer into focus, shed light on certain aspects of xenophobia. It even made phenomena like Venice's ghetto explicable. Was it not inconceivable to have intimate social relationships with, or even to integrate into the community those who refused to honor the Great Mother, the crowned Kami of this little archipelago, in all her manifestations, as Madonna Nicopeia, as the miraculous Virgin of the Miracoli, of Santa Maria Formosa...as the "Kami of Place" in each one of the sestieri? Was she not in her every manifestation the ever-flowing spring from which compassion welled, the Earth Mother to whom to turn in the frightful crises of plague and siege and plunder and rape and birth and death?

In the Orient it is believed that he who invokes Kwan Yin will be invulnerable to the executioner's sword, the adversary's weapons, and will be free of fear in fiercest battle. Isn't it merely sagacious to be at least courteous and reverential to the Kami, the Mediatrix invoked to pray for us in the hour of our death?

12 ❧ *Ponte Dell'Occhio*

In fall no climate is more capricious: Moods change as unpredictably as those of an overwrought matron. The smiling sunshine of the posters, the cobalt-blue skies – photographs lie as bare-facedly as statistics – changes at once to drizzle, fog, squall, to that mild Venetian rain that is so indispensable to release the secret fragrances by which one's nose knows at once it has come home. It needs a degree of rainy humidity to release that olfactory feast of sea-weed, fish heads, iodine, mixed with onions, garlic and oregano, the simmering musty bouquet – pure Yin – of wet mosses, barnacled wood, mildewed leather and old rope, with a waft of tomcat-Yang stirred in.

On these nights of late autumn, when in the silence after dark the houses stand mirroring themselves in the black canals, as in dreams, I roam through the maze of empty streets that are narrow as coffins, not caring where they lead, for they always go somewhere. Yard-wide alleys, pitch-dark sottoportegos – passages tunneled through old buildings – which one would be afraid to enter in any other city, are trustworthy, absolutely safe. Footsteps behind one do not frighten, groups of noisy teenagers heard in the distance do not prompt preventive detours. They pass me by as if I were a ghost. Who would molest a ghost?

The Calle dell'Occhio, just off the Campo San Giacomo dall'Orio, a wraith of an alley, leads to a humped bridge that spans a narrow canal. From the hump, at short distances to right and left two more such high-backed bridges form together with their reflections in the darkened mirror of the canal, perfect circles that are part stone, part dream. A streetlight falls on a stone tablet set in the ancient facade at the end of the bridge. It commemorates an important personage, painter perhaps, or poet. But time has effaced the vines that frame the inscription, every shade of glory with ultimate finality.

Looking up to a lighted window under that tablet, a man, as baldheaded as I, is writing under a bare bulb that hangs from a gilded, coffered ceiling.

He sat there writing by a candle in 1683, in 1783; in 1883 he sat there writing under the shade of a petroleum lamp. Will he still be here in 2083?

All at once, as if hit by an invisible hammer, the black mirror of the canal is shattered. Its fragments become ripples, the ripples change into wavelets, then into waves. The reflections of bridges and houses are pulled apart, torn and pushed into momentary agitations, distortions, that tumble in wild rhythms. A church bell peals in hoarse staccati. It had been wind-still all evening, but suddenly gusts start to blow in from the Adriatic in a fast crescendo of howls, that send the water lapping furiously against the houses.

13   *The Lonely Ones*

Even in gregarious Venice it is possible to be lonely, not with the forlorn isolation that has become part of the human condition in New York, Tokyo or Paris; of humans sequestered, marooned in their cocoons by fright of other humans, in constant fear of exploitation, callous indifference, of violence, rape and murder; suspicious of a courteous word, they panic at an aggressive one.

Here the lonely ones are still oddities, eccentrics deprived by some quirk of temperament, some derangement, from the all-embracing socialization of this city of integrated family clusters spanning three generations in their cozy neighborhoods. Often they compensate for the human closeness they lack by friendship with one of the countless cats that are fed heads and tails of fish, lovingly collected at the fish market by a lonely soul who blends them with some of the daily ration of pasta, spreads the mixture on a piece of Gazettino and puts it where his friend will find it.

Those in whom both humans and cats cause allergic symptoms talk to the canary outside their window in its cage, or to their goldfish in its bowl, unless they are lucky enough to have a mongrel. The rich may have Afghans as an accessory to female seductiveness, or Dobermans to shore up shaky macho; the poor have mongrels simply to love. In the Bar dell'Orologgio an oldish man shares his noon sandwich, literally mouth to mouth, with his semi-poodle. On the Campo San Stin, at midnight, a limping gray-beard tries to play hide and seek with a lethargic more or less German pseudo-shepherd. A dachshund-bulldog synthesis on the Fondamente Ormesini wears home-crafted overshoes of plastic at the lightest sprinkle. Behind the Castelforte San Rocco an old spinster not only feeds pigeons and gulls copiously – every Venetian with a shred of heart left will do that – but talks to them, consoles them in bad weather that "this too shall pass...."

On the disconsolate Fondamente del General Giuliti, a man in a black cashmere coat of old-fashioned cut and a homburg hat stands in the icy wind, pulling slices of white bread out of a pigskin briefcase. The gulls screech around the Victorian figure who stands there muttering genteelly, his face seigniorial but haggard, marked by decades of solitary aloofness. And there are others, withdrawn so deep in their shells of isolation, that they refuse to talk even to a gull, condemning themselves to lifelong soliloquy, from pianissimo to fortissimo.

The old priest on the vaporetto on his way back to his desk at the Cimetero, mumbles his monologue softly in the Doric mode, after so many years among the dead. Other Anchorites argue and harangue in fiercely syncopated diction, as the one I drew on the Fondamente Briati where, behind chicken wire, a Christ weathered to driftwood hangs in his shrine of moldy wood flanked by two stone tablets with the inscription effaced to the riddlesome text: PIE...LARG.DIV.ACIADO.AZIO.E He was in his forties, powerful enough, an athlete run to fat. He stood addressing the large crowd only he could see, whipping up his audience's wrath to fever pitch. His gestures were violent, yet measured, almost elegant and he shouted in dialect, staccato. Not once did he point at the crucifix, hence I took his subject to be not theological

but secular. As I stood drawing him, he suddenly spread his arms, and looking me in the eye, took four rapid steps in my direction. I panicked, quickly closed my sketchbook and shifted my eyes devoutly to the Savior, while calculating options. It was superfluous, for the orator, never aware of me, came to a stop at arm's length and continued his address, allowing me to finish my drawing.

A few hundred yards further, on the Campo San Sebastiano, I met two more lonely ones, but these were chained matrimonially on their island of isolation, their folie à deux, on which they had yelled at each other without pause all their adult life and were destined to continue shouting until death do them part.

Between San Marco and San Moise is the territory of a beggar woman, who runs constantly to nowhere on her knotty legs, in stockings that crinkle around her ankles, her toothless mouth mumbling curses and insults at everyone, cowed benefactors included. Only on the two young carabinieri who guard this elegant stretch does she bestow her hideous toothless grin, which they evade with shy embarrassment, casting down their eyes in recognition of her unalienable right to operate here, a right as legitimate as that of the Winged Lion.

The loner who has his beat at the Ponte dell Arsenale seems to share her dim view of humanity. He is well-dressed and does not beg, nor does he shout. His solo is inaudible, even if his mouth is in violent perpetual motion. With angry thumps and thrusts of his cane, with furious eyes he must be reproaching the tower of San Giorgio Maggiore with some monstrous injustice. San Giorgio, silent and aloof, keeps floating placidly on his island across the wide water.

The youngish fierce-eyed, bearded man who haunts the Piazzetta dei Leoncini, however, sometimes frightens the children, who as dozens of generations of children before them, are riding the teddy-bear lions of red marble. He walks at a brisk pace; then, after a fixed number of strides he stops, turns abruptly on his heels, stands stock still and assumes a striking pose that he can keep almost indefinitely before repeating his run, either adagio or presto according to his demon's command. Only very rarely he utters a volley of sounds. I have also found him in the San Marco circumambulating the Chapel of the Madonna Nicopeia for an hour or so; no one interfered with his ritual. During the Carneval, I am sure, I spotted him under his medieval disguise, although it altered his running phase, which was considerably shortened. After a short jog he climbed on top of the high Proclamation stone, struck his most imperial pose and froze in a splendid sweep of arm. Gradually a great throng gathered, waiting for a second act that never came. He stood there, a silent sculpture in living stone, stood there for so long that when I passed by again, long after my drawing was finished, not a hair had moved. It must have been his all-time record, and he could not stop, feeling at last in full communication with the world.

14 ❧ *Lunchtime*

At twelve-thirty, the grocer puts heavy wooden shutters before his shop window, the luggage seller on his flat feet drags his display of suitcases inside from the sidewalk, the chestnut vendor throws a green tarpaulin over his modest equipment. The lady of the fur shop comes tripping outside on her spike heels, shakes her bleached curls, winds down the iron shutters. At the butcher's the flayed lamb is tenderly deposited in the icebox. At the fish market men in rubber boots are hosing down the stone floors. Old women hurriedly gather fins, tails, fish heads for their cats. Dignified antique dealers, who spend their days reading newspapers amidst polychromed saints, put wire shutters in front of their windows, leaving on the little light, just in case the lady in ocelot, the man in the cashmere coat they have been waiting for, should pass by. But one of the shop owners at the Teatro della Fenice just turns the little sign "Aperto" around, to read "Chiuso." Inside he and his friends are sitting down on the ottocento chairs around the settocento table. The little waiter from next door puts the espressos on it, and the lunchtime round of whist can start.

The campi around Venice's churches were once grassy meadows. On the Campo San Giacomo dell'Orio the grass has disappeared but plenty of good old trees survive to shade the benches where office girls eat their lunch. For all the women of the parish with their babies and toddlers, for the grandmothers on their canes it is still their village green. Here they congregate to smoke and chain-chew caramelli, cackle about the latest fashions, the outrageous prices of pomodori and pepperoni, about the hazards of childbirth, about operations and illicit love, in that bovine peace of mind allowed by the absence of cars that could endanger their

young, the safe distance from the canals they could drown in.

No psychoanalytical data are available on the effect of the campo environment on the behavior patterns of the toddlers of San Giacomo throughout their lifecycle, but careful observation suggests that the females, after an enchanting long-legged puberty, are rapidly converted into statuesque matrons, whose powerful lungs allow them to moo with such force their "Angelo!" or "Mario!" that it carries well beyond the confines of the parish. The males seem to mature into uncomplicated adult infantility, reasonably industrious if unavoidable, docile and peaceful as husbands, and as honest as is expedient in this life. In their later years, they remain touchingly faithful to their campo and the Taverna on the corner of the Rio San Giacomo. Here they exchange life experiences and debate with philosophical mien their childhood to continue their disputations, to spell out the Corriere dell'Sport, or simply to recover from their arduous shuttle between campo and taverna, reclining on the benches under the ancient trees, watching ever new harvests of toddlers grow up into strapping youngsters, precocious virtuosi on the plastic automatic rifle, as their long-legged granddaughters play their recorders.

On the corner of the Ponte di Donna Onesta there is a little restaurant where the omelet is pockmarked but reasonably priced, and adjoining it is the dainty shop, where behind the inspiring window display of lacy raffiné panties and brassieres decorated with butterflies and little hearts, one day I saw two nuns, a stout middle-aged one and a very pale young thing in a white coif, examining an object – I could not make out its precise nature – dangling from the shopkeeper's forefinger. I could not resist jotting it down quickly. Nevertheless, when closing my sketchbook I noticed the little crowd that had gathered behind me just as quickly and discreetly, watching the baldheaded professor with admiration, but not without amusement. This happened in the Street of the Honest Woman.

15 ❧ *Aqua Alta*

At seven, it is still pitch dark, a howl of sirens. A fire? There is no red glow in the sky. At eight, in the sickly dawn, the water in the usually placid Rio Marin below my window is in an uproar, barely an inch under street-level. At half-past, the quays are flooded, the narrow Rio Marin has become a Grand Canal, with wavelets breaking against the walls of Hotel Basilea. A few men in hip-boots come splashing by, lifting their legs high as circus horses in the violent squall that makes shutters rattle, streetlights swing. Plastic bags white, black, sky-blue, bloated with garbage swim past like odd waterfowl bobbing on the bottle green water. The scraggly potted little palms at the front door slowly keel over, try to swim away, but are caught by an elderly gentleman in a homburg hat and yellow hip-boots. Felipe, the busboy, lassoes them from the stoop and Signor Mario runs to the door to bow in gratitude with his finest smile. The old gentleman lifts his hat and wades on. A freight launch with a contingent of executives under umbrellas with their attaché cases passes on its way to the station. The mail man, all oilcloth and plastic, hands over a soaked package of letters.

By then it is ten thirty and the first tourists appear in borrowed gear, slosh past to take snapshots of this entertainment they feel entitled to, deaf to the whispers – still gentle for the time being – by cosmic forces, about the drowning of cities and continents, safely isolated in their capsules of touristic inanity.

A little after noon the streets have become more or less passable in good galoshes, reasonably dry between the puddles. The greengrocer around the corner has opened his basement shop, booted housewives stand choosing escaroles from floating crates. The owner of the furniture shop is drying his mosaic floor between settees and commodes prophylactically placed on blocks. Wading through their labyrinth in boots, the Venetians take the aqua alta in stride as being an integral part of the human condition, swearing a bit and smiling wryly: "Well, at any rate, we don't have avalanches, like the Swiss...."

The afternoon rain makes Venice irresistible: the ochres and siennas of the houses, the grays and sallow whites of marble facades chant in stilled polyphonies. The old-rose brick of the Madonna dell'Orto and San Alvise become lacquered Braque browns and blacks, that glow with inner fervor. On the ledges of the churches the gray pigeons

huddle in the drizzle; now and then, with a whoosh of wing, one detaches itself, dives into the wet grisaille. One never meets "people" in the streets on these days of rain: each one approaching is a Person in his own right. A couple with two little children, each with his own tiny umbrella, splash across the Campo di Frari. The children in their red boots jump across and into black puddles; the man has his free hand around his wife's shoulder, she hers in the belt of his raincoat. They too are happy, humming a song as they disappear in the side entrance of the Frari, where the famous presepio is on display: a miniature manger in a vast constellation of moving comets, stars rising, sheep grazing, wood-cutters sawing, ships plying oceans, complete with red sunset and silvery moonrise, that make these tiny tots squeal in ecstasy as if TV had never been invented.

The cat colony that lives in the Frari's garden is braving the rain to have an early supper of cold spaghetti from soaked newspapers. On days like these Venice becomes an umbrella ballet. One afternoon when it was too wet to draw and too beautiful to stay at home, I classified Venetian streets by their umbrella capacity. First those few, wide enough to accommodate eight umbrellas abreast, like the Via Nuova or Via Garibaldi. Category two comprises all those calles and salizadas where you can negotiate a safe passage provided one of the two umbrella carriers set on a collision course rests the umbrella on his head, while the other holds his as high as he can, in the air. A third category of street requires the approaching pedestrian to close his umbrella, and if he is a perfect gentleman to press himself courteously against the wall. If there are two perfect gentlemen they act similarly, and then it becomes a noble contest in gentility with smiles and "after you" gestures, which is won by the wet loser. In streets of the fourth category even the lone umbrellist folds his device in order not to ruin it. There are a number of these narrow wormholes in the Castello and some, like the Calle Bersana, near San Zanipolo, where one does not have to fear getting wet, even with a rolled up umbrella, for no rain would deign to get caught in these crevices where the leaning facades almost touch.

The lady at the Biennale office, reached by tightrope walking along the temporary footbridges always standing at the ready in sections for instant assembly, confided: "My husband, he is very, very Veneziano! They are so funny, these Veneziani! I am from Vicenza where we do not have trouble with aqua alta. My husband, he keep his bottles in the wine cellar, he refuse to take them upstair! This mornink it was very high tide, was it not, well for the first time his wine got wet. You see, I told him why not take them upstairs? You know what he said, typical Venziano, he said this is an exception, he said, and my bottles they have cork, so what can happen?"

16 ❧ *Horses*

The splendid marble facade of the Ospedale Civile, with its elegant bas-reliefs, was once that of the Scuola di San Marco. It stretches from the Rio dei Mendicante to the front of the thirteenth-century brick church of San Giovanni e Paolo, the Pantheon of the doges and their families. In front of the San Zanipolo, as it is popularly known, stands the compelling equestrian statue of the Condottiere Colleoni, the brilliant mercenary who was just not quite brilliant enough to read the small print of the contract he signed with the Most Serene Republic. It specified that he, Colleoni, would bequeath his considerable assets to it, on condition that his statue would be erected in front of the San Marco. But when, in 1484, Colleoni died, the Council bethought itself that, useful as any addition to its depleted coffers might be, the presence of even a great mercenary on its Piazza was too steep a price to pay. The perfect Venetian solution to the dilemma presented itself: The statue was commissioned, indeed from a great sculptor, the Florentine Verrochio, and according to the agreement it would be placed in front of the San Marco. Not the Basilica, however, but the Scuola di San Marco. Venetians have always been proud of their uprightness, by the rules of their game.

San Zanipolo, showcase of ducal vanity and pride that no death can quench, has through the centuries been protected by brazen Colleoni on his splendid steed, one of the three horses to which the once-crowded Venetian stable is reduced, including the splendid twentieth-century

fable-horse by Marino Marini in front of the Peggy Guggenheim Foundation.

Once, before the wooden bridges were replaced by high-arched stone ones, horses were part of the Venetian cityscape. Now, apart from Colleoni's mount, there only remain two: the one on the Riva degli Schiavoni and the surviving lone bronze horse, once part of the equine quartet that graced the front of the San Marco ever since it was stolen from Constantinople in the thirteenth century, together with the complete center bay of the Basilica's facade. They were Greek horses, probably dating to the fourth to seventh century B.C.E., heavily gilded in their heyday, and they stood there for centuries, a symbol of the Serenissima's glory, until Napoleon pilfered them in his turn, and took them to Paris to adorn his Arc de Triomphe du Caroussel.

Eventually they were returned to their, more or less, rightful owners and to their place on the San Marco, be it without their golden outer skins, which somehow stayed behind in France, to prance in their bronze nudity as nobly, majestically as ever. It took our century of pollution, the fumes of the industries across the bay, to gnaw away the ancient bronze. A few years ago three of the quadrupeds had to be removed, leaving the last survivor a lonely, friendless target for desultory snap shooters.

The third and last Venetian horse stands on the Rivo degli Schiavoni, with Vittorio Emmanuel, end product of another extinct species, the Kings of Italy, on its back, that diminutive little king who stood in Mussolini's shadow on the grandstands, his right arm martially stretched in fascist salute, but with a slight tremor, with sad eyes staring into impending doom. The sculptor has enlarged him considerably to bring him into proportion with his steed and make him swing his sword above his plumed helmet as if it were Excalibur. Ludicrous in sunlight, horse and rider become touching in fog, at dusk.

But returning to that pantheon of past glory, watched over by Colleoni, the Church of San Zanipolo. Immediately to the right of the entrance in an oversized, over-adorned marble conceit rests the skeleton of the Doge Mocenigo, celebrating his once-spectacular feats and superb valor for all eternity, as if glorifying life – high life. The Falier mausoleum, almost next to it, is even more conspicuously brazen: white, cream and yellow marble have been tortured into the trompe l'oeil velvet curtains, tassels, fringes, ropes, frills and cherubs that frame the effigies of the not particularly attractive Doges Falier, senior and junior, bedecked as they are with their ducal finery, as well as Junior's spouse, a well-fed but overdressed dogessa, less woman than assemblage of marble spare parts: curls, ruffles and jewels. The trio is surrounded by a surfeit of theatrically personified Virtues, Victories and other such abstractions that manage to convert a tomb into a spoof on that vainglory, that impudence, to which mortals, if all too rich and powerful, are subject.

Between Mocenigo and Falier the much more modest Bragadin memorial tells such a disgusting story that only in a century like ours that saw the reinstatement of torture as an acceptable auxiliary of power,

one would dare to retell it: Bragadin, the heroic defender of Fumagosta on Cyprus was defeated by the Turks. The Turkish commander guaranteed him safe conduct for the ceremony of handing over the city's keys. When Bragadin appeared with his retinue of officers in their gala uniforms, the Pasha, pretending to become incensed, accused Bragadin of having put Moslem prisoners to death, had the entire delegation hacked to pieces then and there, except for poor Bragadin for whom worse was in store. After his nose and ears were cut off, he was driven through the streets for ten consecutive days carrying heavy loads and forced to his knees to kiss the ground in front of the Pasha's palace. Finally he was flayed alive and his skin, stuffed with straw, was suspended as a trophy from the bowsprit of the Turkish flagship on its home voyage.

The most modest, most human of all these mausoleums is that of Doge Vendramin, whose palazzo nowadays fulfills the function of municipal casino. His tomb has an effigy of the ruler peacefully asleep, in quiet dignity. Art historians, however, derogate it bitterly as a "mere façade," because the doge has no back, as if a back were such an indispensable part of a dead doge's anatomy.

San Zanipolo's boastful grandiloquence preaches a

melancholy sermon about religion, when it condemns itself to subvert its mission, to betray its rootedness in the full, divine humanity of its Founder, when it allies itself with the worldly power of the Prince of this World, falling precisely for that temptation He rejected when He ordered Satan to get behind him.

Neither the lovely fifteenth-century rosette window in Zanipolo's South wall, nor its treasury of masterworks by Bellini, Lotto and Vivarini, compensate for the malaise all this dead ostentation provokes. But in the dark sacristy, much too high on the wall, hangs a large dark canvas of which the central figure is such a luminous female of flesh and blood, that all the pompous dead doges are at once forgotten. By far the sexiest lady she is, ever seen even in Venetian religious art, where Eros and Agape are so inextricably mixed together. Her face is veiled, but no veil can contain the passion, the rapture of her aroused eyes, the ecstasy with which her lovely dimpled arm embraces the large cross. Not only the doges next door, even the Baroque histrionics of the figures with whom she shares the picture-plane evaporate instantly in such fervor.

The doddering attendant in his black alpaca jacket recalled the painting to be by Jacopo Bassano, seicento, but no, *mi dispiace,* no photograph was ever available. As he stood squinting at it, trying to recall the painting's title, a young, tall monk in spotless white crossed the Sacristy.

"Could you tell me, Father, who is that lovely saint?"

"*Vous parlez francais?*" he asked.

"*Alors, voyez vous, cher monsieur, ce n'est pas une sainte! Evidemment, n'est-ce pas, c'est La Foi!* Obviously that is no saint, it is Faith. Is not Faith precisely like this? Does not Faith see the world as through a veil? Do not its arms embrace our Savior's cross? *Alors, voila!*"

"*Ah, merci, mon Père,*" I said, looking him in the eye, "it is so very moving, so deeply touching."

"*Très, très touchant!*" he agreed, with a little smile that was almost a wink and as he finished his arrangement of liturgical laundry on the shelves, he glanced back a few times, still smiling.

I walked out of San Zanipolo, crossed the campo. On the narrow Ponte Rosso I had to circumvent a couple in profound embrace. I mumbled, "Permesso!" The girl shot a glance in my direction.

I knew that face! Where had I seen it? Then, from the next little bridge came gay little cataracts of laughter and at once I remembered: It was La Foi.

17 ❧ Ars Longa, Vita Brevis

In their improvised role of art historian they stand, guidebook at the ready, commenting on masterpieces for their audience of yawning wives and yearning daughters. They can't stop pontificating in German, in French, in Oxford, Cockney or Brooklyn English. They trudge from Accademia to Museo Correr for their next performance, in competition with professional polyglot guides who know it all by heart. They gallop from thirteenth-century Paolo Veniziano, via steely Mantegna and tender Bellinis to Tiepolo's airborne angels and goddesses, and come to a solemn moment's full stop at a Titian. The Carpaccios have to wait until this afternoon so let's hurry up, for the preluncheon schedule still includes Titian's "Assumption of the Virgin" at the Frari, plus an acre of Tintorettos at the Scuola San Rocco. According to reliable worldwide statistics, the average time allotted to the certified Grade A masterpieces – is seven seconds.

To see a painting, to respond to it in my way, I have to stand in front of it on the very spot where once the painter stood. I stand there scribbling on my sketchpad. I do not pretend to "copy" the painting. I try to enter into contact with it, to converse – most humbly – with its maker. Sometimes I succeed and the conversation yields both delight and revelation.

At other times the conversation splutters and stops: We don't understand each other's language. Tintoretto apparently did not labor to please me, but those who in 1564 made him the winner of a competition to decorate the new Scuola di San Rocco. For twenty years he worked on it, and the stupendous "Crucifixion" is its apotheosis. John Ruskin found it "beyond analysis and praise," hence worthy of its presence in the Scuola as "one of the three most precious buildings of Italy," with the Sistine Chapel and Pisa's Campo Santo.

Still, each time I come away from San Rocco I am oppressed by my inadequacy, my inability to be touched by these Tintorettos. Bowled over as I am by their wizardry, I am powerless to establish contact with, to relate to this awesome oeuvre, to see it as "religious" art. The little Memlinc in the Accademia moves me as deeply as the Dirk Bouts in the Museo Correr. I would not swap these two little canvases for all Venetian "religious" painting that came after Bellini.

I find it odd that these Venetian painters seem so programmed with the spasmodic saints and operatic heroes of biblical and antique mythology, that they were blinded to the glory of their vast skies over sandbank islets barely above the water line. Even Canaletto and Guardi dismissed what a van Goyen, a Seghers, a Van de Velde would have celebrated: this splendor of "things as they are," of water and mist and cloud, with the tall barely leaning Campanile of Burano piercing the cloud deck, the sea marshes of Torcello in the distance, grasses and reeds blowing, waterfowl bobbing and diving, a lonely rowboat in the immense space, the golden dusk.

Could it be a cultural incompatibility? For I grew up in awe of

those Flemish "primitives," those fourteenth-century painters as Van Eyck, Van der Weyden or Breughel. They were my aesthetic eye openers. Even throughout the seventeenth century, that Golden Age of Dutch mercantile and military power, the art of the Lowlands remained an art stilled, introverted, whether its subject matter was "religious" or secular. The backdrop of those Flemish religious paintings have something in common with the chaste interiors of De Hoogh, Terborgh and of course Vermeer: that clarity of the eye that makes it "the candle of the body." Each one of these secular paintings is an epiphany. Our landscape painters, Hobbema, Van Goyen, Seghers and Ruysdael, as were the Chinese Sung painters, nature mystics for whom sky, water, earth and light, invited contemplation. Each one of Rembrandt's late portraits witnesses to the centrally human, affects me "religiously" so much deeper than all Venetian Crucifixions and Resurrections together. His biblical subjects, his "Christ at Emmaus," are free from all histrionics. The event is an inward one, its light is the "Light no darkness can overcome."

Rubens, among the painters of the Lowlands, seems to be an exception in his lusty brilliance. But even he, in the portraits of his wife, Helene Fourment, for instance, sees as with a shudder beyond the blooming of flesh, its transitoriness. His "Last Judgment" in the Pinakothek of Munich, that stupendous cascade of human bodies, is less an acrobatic extravaganza than the vision of a cosmic calamity. The light in these Tintorettos is magical and haunting, but remains alien to my eye; it suggests the stage. The ineffable light in a Vermeer, while not the light of everyday, is not foreign at all: It is the Light one has glimpsed at moments of grace, touching a face. Tintoretto's, Veronese's, Tiepolo's human figures move in perfect choreographies of which the immense hormonal vitality forces one to puzzle about the mysterious relationship between body and spirit. It is as if in Venetian art the emotional display, the operatic grandiloquence shocks me into numbness.

"The Doge Grimani adoring Faith" in the Palazzo Ducale is the title of an enormous, sumptuous canvas that epitomizes a religion that has become all too esoteric, this pantomime of devotion: a jumbo cross flies through the sky, accompanied by squadrons of angels. Human forms on the ground and in the air posture in stereotyped holy calisthenics, flail arms and legs, flaunt beards and breasts – garlands and veils chastely hiding the tabooed loins – around an all too pious doge in the prescribed stance of exophthalmic rapture.

In the Hall of the Grand Council, all walls covered by scenes of mayhem, martyrdom, glory and the flattery of power, a pride of youngsters in neon-green and pink plastic jackets and moon boots erupt in a wild rock dance on the parquet floor under the coffered golden ceiling.

Veronese once sinned against the Church's taboos by painting a dog in his "Last Supper": no dogs allowed in such a holy scene! Veronese did not have to chase the pooch. He simply changed the title to "Feast in the House of Levi," where dogs were not prohibited. There was no objection.

The Museo dell Arte Moderna is housed in the Ca Pesaro, Longhena's swan song. It is more than a museum: It's a fascinating sampler of all that has happened to the "fine" arts over the past hundred years. One wanders from nineteenth-century Salon paintings, past more or less brilliant Impressionists and Post-Impressionists, shrill Fauves, oscillating Pointillists, cerebral Cubists, frantic Futurists, exhibitionistic Surrealists, raw Expressionists, to be dizzied by that entire avalanche of schools, movements, idiosyncrasies and fads that since Cézanne and, until today, have fallen one over the other with ever increased acceleration. It is indispensable to study this collection, to make one realize how fast the exciting dernier cri converts itself into a dull déjà vu, how little remains of all the sound and fury of avant-gardes and manifestos, how dated so much looks barely a decade after it was so formidably fashionable.

Idols of the Italian post-war scene, Campigli, Cassinari and Afro, already look as unexciting as they must have been when they were oven-fresh. This art safari confirms that what through the years retains the power to delight, to touch, does so by strict authenticity coupled with sound craftsmanship: a wondrously sensitive still-life by De Pisis, a series of superb etchings by a forgotten American, James McBey, who worked in Venice around the turn of the century; and from that same period the exquisitely tender and mysterious portrait heads modeled in wax by Medardo Rosso, and the haunting, ten-inch high head of a boy by Rik Wouters, that lovable Flemish painter-sculptor who died during World War I.

These draw me back to the Ca Pesaro again and again as do those masterly nineteenth-century portraits by Wilhelm Leibl, Favretto and Antonio Mancini's joyous, lyrical, lovable portrait of his father, a florid Victorian with white moustache, and a nosegay of white and crimson impasto, thrown violently, but precisely on target, on a gleaming black background.

There is also a canvas by that wonderful, dreamy colorist Antonio Music, who here had to throw a heap of emaciated, mutilated corpses on raw linen in blacks, ochres and fuliginous whites, in order to witness to his concentration-camp ordeal, exorcising the beastly evil of our entire epoch. There is a great wealth here of such signs of unmutilated humanness amidst all the super-annotated trivia and frivolities, the disarray of spirit: splendid bronzes by Emilio Greco and Marino Marini, Manzu's heretic cardinals, Augusto Murer's tortured victims of violence, all these authentic works of art witness to the human spirit, prove that tons of ephemeral trash must be produced, framed, put on pedestals, awarded prizes and medals in order to let a Murer, a Favretto or a Manzu speak out in their Vox Humana, one Medardo Rosso, wise and humble, noble enough to choose as ephemeral a medium as wax, to glorify a dewdrop world.

18 ❧ *Intermezzo on Terra Firma*

It takes a few days in this world outside of our world to allow one's senses to be born afresh, to let the dulled ear, the jaded eye become sensitized once again to the splendors of light, the sounds of silence. But all too soon, one begins to take the miracle almost for granted. When that happens – usually after a week or two in Venice – it is wise to interrupt one's stay and to return for a short intermezzo to the mainland. All one has to do is to cross the Giardino Papadopoli, that little oasis of old trees, then climb over a bridge or two to the Piazzale Roma, and instantly one is back in the twenty-first century in all its techno glory. Buses, touring cars complete with TV and WC, roar past, rancorous taxis hoot, paranoid drivers, eyes bulging, must pass the too slow idiot in front. After an average of twenty minutes, nostalgia usually becomes strong enough to make one hurry across the little bridges in the opposite direction, fully renewed for another week of pure perception – eye and ear reborn.

On a recent safari to the Piazzetta, I did not even need twenty minutes, for hardly had I set foot on terra firma when I heard a loud bang and the shattering of glass. Its front end badly mauled, its rear legs on the sidewalk, stood an ancient Fiat, spotted gray and leprously rusty in its terminal misery. Of the aggressor there was no more trace, but its owner stood next to it in piteous dejection. A police car shrieked to a stop. Two uniformed men started the international ritual of removing their heavy leather gloves in extra slow motion.

The proprietor of the late Fiat started a bitter denunciation of his incognito assailant, as the Law stood staring into the far distance. The stout older officer's tranquilizing gestures failed predictably; the left hand of the wronged man clutched the cop's lapel in a firm grip, his knees flexed, his face in supplication turned to heaven. Job's left hand in Chapter Seven must have held the Jahweh's lapel like that.

At last the younger policeman, taking the initiative, removed the hand from his superior's lapel. The Fiat's mourner buried his face in his hands and for some long seconds stood shaken by sobs, but suddenly he threw his head back in a hideous roar of sarcastic laughter, and let it at once drop back on his chest, his arms spread as in a crucifixion, while delivering some lines in adagio espressivo. The sergeant, during this slow movement, pulled a notebook from his breast pocket, licked a yellow pencil stub, and left the dialogue to his junior, concentrating on his writing.

But the victim fell silent and stood there crying quietly. His mute tears were more than the younger cop could stand. I saw him remove his cap with the gleaming visor and go slightly to his knees, pleading with the owner of the deceased, by now a picture of misery himself, very close to tears. The words he spoke escaped me, but they must have been magnificent, for the two dozen people who had watched the drama from the first act and like a Greek chorus commented on every scene, were deeply moved and murmured what sounded like a requiem.

Other Fiats and Alphas stopped dead in their tracks to witness the tragedy, their passengers lurched forward like sacks of flour. Behind all windshields on the Piazzale Roma faces glared in homicidal fury; the blare of horns was deafening.

Across the Rio Foscari Canaletto houses stood in their detached dreams. As I crossed the bridges in the falling dusk a luminous mist was rising. Once in the narrow alley, I first heard a little dog yapping behind a door, then a child practicing scales on a tinny piano. Behind me dragged a limping step in slippers, but from around the corner came the click-click of high heels, of trim, slim legs stepping firmly, and then, from a doorway I heard, really, I swear, clearly the sound of a kiss. I have seen people kiss in many cities, but only in Venice, repeatedly, I have heard their kisses. Faulty technique? Unlikely. Must be a matter of acoustics.

19 🎭 *Buon Natale*

When the summer season has ebbed at last – it may drag on until mid-October – the hotel people heave a deep sigh. The herds in Bermuda shorts and Hawaiian shirts are no longer driven from Ca d'Oro to San Rocco, from Piazza to Murano. Young couples keep coming, on their first outing together, and old couples on their last, longing to recoup their temps perdu, but the frenzy is over.

Logically the season should stay dead until the crocuses raise their heads in the giardini. The hard-nosed Tourist Office would then have had to invent some attractions to take up the slack, as recently it had the inspiration to resurrect the ancient revelries of the Carnevale that had slumbered in suspended animation since the days of Napoleon Bonaparte, but which since 1980 again attracts tens of thousands of innocents, willing to risk in mid-February a terminal Mardi Gras pleurisy in all the jollification. Lord Byron was romantically shocked by the demise of Venetian bellicosity, when he cried out in 1817:

> *Oh, Venice! Venice!*
> *When thy marble walls*
> *are level with the water*
> *there shall be a cry of nations o'er thy sunken halls*
> *a loud lament among the sweeping sea!*
> *If a Northern wanderer weep for thee,*
> *what will thy sons do?*
> *Nothing but weep,*
> *and yet they only murmur in their sleep*
> *in contrast with their fathers....*

The fathers might well have been quite impressed with their progeny's astuteness in thinking up alternatives to rowing galleons and fighting Turks. But no such tours de force are needed to enliven an unprofitable lull around Christmas. Without any incentives the tourists flock to Venice spontaneously, huddled in layers of wool, goose down and animal skins. The reception clerks stand frowning behind their desks, nodding their "Niente!" hands spread in mock commiseration. Every bed is occupied and, since there is nothing else to do, they creak with uncommon frequency. Theaters and movie houses are closed until January fourth; some of the churches even send God on vacation.

In the Merceria the crowds shuffle in dense formations. To be moved by this mass of human bodies induces a kind of elation while watching the stream being pushed toward one, wondering at each of these fellow leaves drifting past on their way to the waterfall, soon to tumble over, slowly, yet all too fast. For each face, a secret to be solved, is hardly glimpsed. Mosaics of karma drift by, with traces of Mongol and Berber, Viking and Hun. Chins jut or recede, noses turn up concavely, curve down as aquiline beaks attempt to combine both. And all those eyes! Bulging eyes, eyes withdrawn in deep sockets, eyes squinting, eyes calling for attention, eyes that see nothing, lifeless, merely reflecting the yellow light of the shop windows...and all these hearts, still beating for a while.

There is no rush in this contented bovine shuffling, with heads slowly swiveling from right to left, left to right, toward other heads, toward things in shop windows. Tempting, useless. Things to hang around one's carcass, to nail provisionally against the walls of one's temporary shelter, to clutter rooms and closets. Things that will impress, arouse envy. Wonderful things one simply must

buy. For suddenly a shuffle quickens, a woman crosses the current of slow-moving flesh to gape at such a thing, a transfixing thing, irresistible, that must be bought, quickly, from which the wrapping is torn in the street, to finger it, to touch it tenderly, with eyes shining. The thing is shown triumphantly to one's companion, just as its enchantment has already begun to wane imperceptibly. In the hotel room the treasure is really unwrapped, turned around on the bed, smiled at: "It is lovely, isn't it, and such a fantastic bargain compared with.... Wouldn't it make a splendid present for him, for her, for them...after all they did for us...?"

At the end of the Rio dei Mendicante that flanks the Ospedale Civile there is one of those little wharves where gondolas and leaking rowboats are repaired in normal times. But this is Christmastime and the most Venetian of all presepios is moored here: a crude hut of plastic sheeting stretched over rough beams nailed to a raft. And in it a life-size papier-mâché Saint Joseph, with a comically elongated torso sits on his nonexistent knees under his monkish cloak, his face all astonishment and rapture, bent over the Bambino in its wicker basket. Mary's head under her sky-blue veil must once have stood in a shop window in the good old days when the mannequins were still sweet young things with forget-me-not eyes, long blond eyelashes and a little cupid mouth. Two female figures, saintly but apocryphal, whose yellow and purple nylon robes trail in the water, complete this extended Holy Family, which waltzes wildly on the waves each time an ambulance launch roars by. It is, however, well secured on its raft with steel cables. The Holy Family may get soaked; it never capsizes.

Butcher shops have looked for at least a week as if all the edible animal kingdom has been massacred in anticipation of the birth of the Lamb of God in His manger. The absence of both ox and ass in the floating presepio on the Rio Mendicante can perhaps be explained: They too were sacrificed in this holocaust, together with all the chickens, turkeys, grouse, pheasants, partridges, geese, ducks and little songbirds that hang naked from hooks, collars of multihued feathers left around their necks by way of tasteful decoration. Wild boar and gentle calf, suckling pig and baby lamb – yes, Agnus Dei – hang quartered in the windows, severed heads delicately holding lemons between jaws pried open.

In the Pescheria, salmon, tuna, lobster and swordfish lie in state, on biers of seaweed. Crabs, shrimp, prawns, eels, squid are dumped in pink and silvery mounds. Here and there a leg, a claw, a fin is still moving. Trout, carp, cod, skate, bass and whiting, mouths agape, are displayed in artful compositions on cracked ice. Kyrie eleison....

Christmas Eve, the wet streets are empty. Everything is closed. Some trattorias have seven-course menus pasted on their windows in the hope of catching the orphaned tourist, segregated tonight, when Venetians celebrate *en famille*. A bar on the Rio Trovaso is still open for a grappa against the damp chill. I just begin to sip it when they come in to pose for me, the heavy-set woman in her white fox collar who must flirt at once with any catchable eye, the other one in pastel mink and gold spike heels whose face is set to judge whatever life has in store as if a personal insult, and their two husbands, one florid in a camelhair coat, the other wiry, whose function it is to neigh loudly each time the fat one cracks a joke, his chin trembling. The teenage daughter stands moping in isolationist protest, wincing at the chatter; the spasms of laughter disturb her new hormonal dreams. Buon Natale! Buon Natale!

The Midnight Mass will be nationally broadcast. Priests in vestments, shuffling microphones, are shooed away by men in dark sunglasses dragging cables. Important personages blinking in the quartz lights are shown with smiling subservience to the VIP section by figures in cassocks and albs. Two little girls in long white dresses come running through the nave to join the children's choir waiting in the aisle, check themselves, and run back to dip their little hands in the holy water, crossing themselves with lightning speed, hopscotching back to their fellow angels in the choir.

Santa Maria Gloriosa di Frari's every corner is bathed in the brightest of light. Titian's over-decorated mausoleum and that of the sculptor Canova are so harshly lit that their occupants would have sat up straight in their tombs — had they been home — sure the Last Judgment had begun. Both were not. For the pyramid-shaped tomb of Canova, with its suggestive half-open door, never contained his body, which was buried in his native village of Posagno. Only the sculptor's heart was placed in this monstrous tomb which Canova did not design for himself but for Titian, who still found it insufficiently grandiose to house what one day would remain of him, and replaced it by his own design, ornamented like a merry-go-round. But what remained of Titian was very little, and was never laid to rest in this tomb, for it too is empty. The great painter was almost a hundred years old when he died of the plague. His body was burned unceremoniously with hundreds of other bodies for fear of contagion. Centuries later an Austrian emperor had Titian's design executed at last, and the truth was discovered: The painter had been given a funeral with all the honors to which such a great man was entitled, except that the coffin intended for the pompous tomb was found to contain nothing but a rock, placed there a few hundred years ago to fool the pallbearers. The inscription on the mausoleum had to be changed to read: *"Benche senza tracie della mortale spoglie del pittore,"* without a trace of the painter's remains.

The klieg lights are moved through the hollow church, and sweep over sepulchres, the bas reliefs of prophets, the carved choir stalls with their dazzled, blinking occupants, finally to come to rest on the sanctuary. TV cameras on their gun carriages wheel into position. Below Titian's "Assumption of the Virgin," lit by massive candlepower to overwhelming gaudiness, the choir intones a hymn, more Sinatra than Palestrina in style. Priests in magnificent chasubles join in, bellowing this nonmusic into their chrome mikes, in the name of the "Padre et Filio et Spirituo Sancto" as a loud baritone asserts. The time has come to seek edification elsewhere.

The city is mute, empty. The water in the canals is high, and laps nervously against the houses. Hasn't someone mentioned a Midnight Mass in the San Marco? I hurry through deserted alleyways where assassins in black capes ought to lie in wait under dark loggias, in deep doorways. In the Calle del Cappellar: a piercing yell. A large man, walking fast, hunched in his greatcoat comes around the corner. A few houses ahead he presses himself

against the wall.

"Permesso!" I stutter, shivers down my spine.

"Prego!" says the assassin. *"Buona notte! Buon Natale!"* The moaning continues. In the Calle dei Botteri a little tiger cat and a ginger tom, absorbed in each other's beauty, are singing their love duet. The usually crowded Rogo Orifice, Shylock's street of the jewelers, at the foot of the Rialto bridge, is deserted. Through the desolate Merceria a few tourists, cameras dangling, still trudge through the thin sleet. In the distance, under the Clock tower, some people stand bunched, as if watching a spectacle. The San Marco, for the fourth time in this one week, lies as a surrealist shipwreck, mirrored in the black water that makes the Piazza into a large square pond. The water, across the Piazza, sloshes between the columns of San Theodore and the Winged Lion, all the way to the island of San Giorgio Maggiore, a faint glimmer of light on an endless black lagoon.

At midnight a hoarse church bell starts to peal: San Pantaleon's, if I recognize it correctly. Then all at once all the bells of all two hundred churches, the bronze tenors, sopranos, baritones and contraltos join in until a choir, a hymnody of tolling, ringing, rolling, clanging, chiming and ding-donging swells into an ecstasy of percussion, that echoes against the wet hollow walls. Has perhaps the Child that must redeem this blood-soaked planet, despite all, been born at last?

The church of the Carmini stands open. Its pillars are dressed up in jackets of dull burgundy cloth that make its dank darkness lugubrious. A voice, deadly tired and old, drones a sermon. Young couples tip-toe in, sketch a desultory genuflection, slip out again into the slow, wet snowfall.

On Christmas morning a shroud of white velvet covers the campo. A row of footprints runs diagonally across it, large footprints, far too large for a dog. They might be a lion's and if so it can only be those of the largest among the tribe of Venetian lions, the Lion of Piraeus at the Arsenale, broken loose this Christmas night after a thousand years of bored captivity, to prowl through the empty city till daybreak. In the deserted streets, with here and there a new plastic automatic weapon rattling, all espresso bars are closed, until I find on the Campo San Barnaba a bar where a few people stand shivering over their coffee, peeling the cellophane off cup-cakes. A wizened derelict is strumming his plastic banjo desperately. The ill-smelling crone is too drunk to take up the collection, and she staggers out through the slush, sinking down with her glass of vino on the wet steps of San Barnaba, emptying it angrily, smashing it on the flagstones.

On this Christmas morning the great, gold crowned Madonna of the Carmini in her real lace finery, bedecked with strings of pearls, amethysts and rhinestones, stands listening to the choir of little children, conducted by a buxom old nun, singing an endless Maria hymn. Full of grace she stands there, her beautiful eyes of glass under the long silken lashes smiling down, the Life Giver, the Kami of this place.

20 ❧ *Lavallière*

The silver-haired man who joined me at my table said "Permesso" with a courteous, formal bow as if wishing to identify himself as being a gentleman. He wore a threadbare dark gray Harris tweed coat, combined with the flowing black bow tie that in the nineteenth century signaled its wearer to be an artist. I had not seen such a lavallière since in Arles I sketched the statue of Frédéric Mistral, great poet of the Provence, who wears it combined with a flambard, a wide-brimmed black felt hat for extra swagger. The old man across the table sat watching me read the Gazettino and was obviously waiting for it.

The espresso machine, still the old-fashioned nickel urn with the eagle on top, was sputtering and spitting. The owner's wife was trying to pacify it, for the padrone himself was busy scraping the Christmas decorations off the window with a razorblade, trying to save every gold star for the children who stood watching him tensely. The largest star, marvelously intact, he gave to a tiny girl with pigtails, who stuck it on her forehead and took off in a little gavotte that almost made her airborne, for Tiepolo's influence is still strong in Venice.

The woman behind the bar stood clicking her tongue with those almost too intimate little cries of delight that are quite normal here: One is not expected to hide one's feelings whether one has them or not. Men may weep in public, women may yell "Mario!" out of their windows with all the passion, panic, fury of hormonal surplus. Neither upper nor lower lip is praised for being held stiff; we are not in Aberdeen here.

The old man smiled courteously, when at last the Gazettino was his. It must have been his flowing lavallière that flashed me back to my hometown on the Belgian border, long before one reached it over parkways. There were few cars in those days. The judge drove a Minerva with a body of deep brown teakwood and a brass radiator. Our doctor had his chauffeured black Panhard. The son of the paper mill owner roared through town in his Bugatti Torpedo, irresistible to the girls. The old houses across the Campo San Stin were the doubles of the ones I passed on my way to school, each one with a face of its own: benevolent, mysterious or evil and mean, their pretentious balconies slightly out of whack.

As to the lavallières: Our house painter Mijnheer Sondijker wore one, combined with the black flambard on his gray curls. On Sundays he stood behind his easel on the old city wall painting his naïve cityscapes, striking a pose like that of the tall figure on the left of Rembrandt's "The Cloth Guild (*De Staalmeesters*)." Mijnheer Gemmeke, my grandfather's old schoolmate, a bank teller, turned up his waxed moustache under his aquiline nose, donned riding boots with spurs, and on Sunday mornings mounted his black steed, Troki, rented from van Boom's stable. Ramrod stiff in his saddle, he turned at once into the general he was at heart. Not a Dutch general with a head like an Edam cheese, nor a monocled German blockhead. No, he became the Generale della Rovere-Grimaldi, eagle-faced hero of the battle of Ventimiglia, his hat at a rakish angle, his white beetle brows all a-bristle. I had the honor of being his aide de camp on chestnut-hued old Flora from the same stable who, noble as was the curve of her neck, was a little stiff in the hindquarters as she was seven years my senior. Together we stepped through town, greeting the by now long-deceased church-goers with our riding crops, tactfully avoiding both familiarity and condescension. We cantered through the outskirts, until just across the Belgian border we galloped down the bridle paths on the estate of our friend the Prince de Mérode, who, alas, we never had a chance to thank for his absentee hospitality, as he lived in Brussels or his Monaco villa.

Often the third in our party was Jon Fey, who had been mayor of my native village of St. Pieter before it was brutally annexed by Maastricht. He was a bachelor, and with his long nose and skeptically raised eyebrows doubled as the Venetian baker on the Rio Marin. Jon was indeed a skeptic, who believed in nothing but himself as a horseman and superb hunter, and perhaps a little in the Virgin Mary, for a polychromed Madonna stood on his mantelpiece. He always wore greenish tweed plus-fours with khaki

gabardine leggings, and was rarely seen without two dachshunds frolicking around these leggings, or without a shotgun over his shoulder. I felt such awe and envy of those elegant leggings that I asked him to give me shooting lessons. He let me practice on a target tacked on the outhouse in his backyard.

I might have become a great hunter, if my training had not almost turned into tragedy. For Jon's housekeeper, Katrina, with her dark moustache and reddish pompadour, had retired there before my lesson started, so that my bullet almost pierced her! It was to be the end of my career as a hunter, in fact, the last time I fired a weapon, even at an outhouse. Distressing as it would have been to have slain Katrina, how much more depressing I felt it was to kill innocent rabbits, however handsome the leggings that went with it.

These were the ghosts that loomed up in the bar on the Campo San Stin. Their counterparts I found still surviving here. I saw them on Sundays coming down from their fifth-floor walk-ups, having shed their disguise of waiter or luggage repairman, meticulous in form-fitting cashmere coats with velvet collars and polished shoes, to become at last the country squire, the Parisian boulevardier that only they knew was their true identity. Last survivors of that extinct species: the man of distinction!

The old gentleman across from me must have dreamed of being both great artist and man of distinction. He began to talk, when he had finished his paper and a double vino bianco, about the aqua alta.

"Naturally," he said, "all through our history we Veniziani have been a bit nervous about sinking into the sea. But we had no choice. The Gospel we respect may recommend to build one's house on rock: We had no rock, all we had was mud and sand.... And yet, by the grace of God, you must admit that we are still above the waterline – most of the time. And if you go around the corner to the Scuola San Giovanni Evangelista, you'll see the American 'Save Venice Committee' and that is especially reassuring: Those Americans will not allow us to sink! They cannot afford it! They need us, not only as a set for their movies, they need us for their prepaid tours. Where would they be, with calamari swimming through the Danieli, the Gritti Palace, the American Express and Harry's Bar? Tell me! Bah!"

He got up stiffly, and after a courteous bow of the correct variety, left for his lone attic.

But perhaps it was less lonely than I assumed, for a few days later I seemed to recognize the worn tweed coat from the back as it crossed the Piazza. It was not alone.

21 ❧ *Carnevale*

In the seventeenth and eighteenth century, its power in steep decline, the Serenissima was enjoying herself, celebrating her bedevilment with magnificence. It was around this time that the Grand Tour was invented. For the nobility and patrician intelligentsia of Europe a pilgrimage to Italy, and to Venice in particular, became part of a European — especially British — upper-class education. With the Grand Tour, tourism was born and only had to evolve into prepaid package tours. It was in this era also that the extravagant, prolonged Carnevale stretched over the

better part of the year, and it became Europe's first and irresistible tourist attraction. And Venice had more to offer to these early tourists: seven opera theaters, brilliant painters and superb composers like Monteverdi, Marcello and Vivaldi. Its great art collections, concerts, splendid libraries and the unrivalled splendor of Venetian pageantry charmed the sophisticates. Regattas, bullfights, pig-racing, brothels and gambling dens drew the less refined. The Queen of the Sea had become the purveyor of entertainment, and of a bawdiness that shocked Shelley into writing: "I had no conception of the excess to which avarice, cowardice, superstition, ignorance, passionless lust and all the brutalities which degrade human nature could be carried, until I had passed a few days in Venice."

The licentiousness, protected by anonymity was facilitated by the wearing of the usually chalk-white characteristic mask, the tabarro, the wide cape that concealed all bodily form, and the baula, the black veil that went with it. To recognize someone thus disguised was a taboo, a serious social gaffe. Prolonged peace, limitless love of pageantry, luxury, avid sensualism announced Venice's final undoing. Her institutions, often called tyrannical, although probably the most humane and democratic of their time, had crumbled. Her constitution, for centuries guarantor of her oligarchic structure, had become calcified. Napoleon dealt the Most Serene Republic its death blow and with it put an end to that strangest of social phenomena, the half-year-long Carnevale.

In 1980 it was resurrected, for purely economical reasons. On a chilly Sunday in February at noon, the Bersaglieri opened the twice-born Carnevale in the Piazza with a concert of remarkable dissonance. Middle-aged men they were, in military uniforms that time had allowed to become a little tight at the waist, their heads almost hidden under the flat Bersaglieri hats adorned with more black and blue-green rooster feathers than ever grew on even the cockiest rooster's tail. They specialized in strangely hurried, old-fashioned march tunes, and when at last they

left the bandstand, they marched away in the semi-gallop that Bersaglieri tradition demands.

In this curious accelerated locomotion they ran along the Riva di Schiavoni blowing their tunes, dashingly, breathlessly, in shrill falsettos. Never allowing themselves to slow down, they either galloped in time with the prestissimo "umpahumpah" of the tuba and the strident staccato of the trumpets, or stood still, panting heavily. For each time they reached the foot of one of the many bridges on the Riva they stopped dead, stood at attention trying to catch their breaths, before starting their run once more, up and down the steep steps, blowing desperately a tempo, their plump behinds following on their heels, continuing their mad rush nonstop, until, as abruptly, they stood gasping for air at the next bridge. At the Caffe Bella Vista, where they were expected, they sank down heavily on the chairs, gasping, attempting to revive themselves with large pitchers of vino bianco, emptied at once and quickly refilled. Only partly recovered, they lifted themselves, stood around for a while, strutting martially for the benefit of their following of admirers that had managed to keep up with them. After a last quick swig of wine, almost fully restored, they fell into formation, raised their brasses and started their suicidal gallop once more, cock feathers flying, dissonants wheezing.

Near the Campo San Stefano, at the steep bridge over the Rio Corner, an old man came stiffly shuffling out of a doorway, his thin body wrapped in an eighteenth-century coat of watered silk, a white lace jabot neckpiece and sky-blue silk knickers. He wore a plumed tricorn hat, a sword with a golden grip dangled at his side. Fragile as a Meissen figurine he shuffled on red patent leather shoes, his face elegantly bony, sallow and powdered, his wig spotlessly white. Slowly he climbed the steep steps, then, on the hump of the bridge, recognizing two ladies in furs, he turned on his high heels and supporting himself on his tall cane, bowed deeply with a wide swing of the plumed hat. They stood there, exchanging compliments and polite grimaces, as if it was the most normal thing in the world. It was! For the old gentleman, on this first evening of the Carnevale, had simply allowed himself to be the Venetian patrician he had in his own mind always been, and acted it out in perfect naturalness. Once more he bowed, replaced with delicate care the tricorn on his wig, and continued his stroll through his private dream city.

If the Lord were as merciful as advertised, He would let him take a rest on a bench behind the Teatro della Fenice, gently lull him to sleep, to wake up in the rococo section of heaven for all eternity.

On the Piazza meanwhile the Carnevale was reaching its paroxysm. The most powerful sound systems ever made had been commandeered to produce the ultimate in electronic din, so that the Campanile seemed to sway, and a repetition of the disaster of 1902, when it fell flat on its face, seemed imminent. It was all still improvised in 1980. Many more visitors had flocked to Venice than expected, hungry for relief from the tensions of a paranoid world of terrorism, violence and the continued threat of Armageddon, a world in which the colossal is in total power. They had come to enjoy themselves, perhaps a last time. They had no spectacular costumes, but turned their jackets inside out, smeared their faces with grease paint, converted pantyhose and improvised tutus into prima ballerina outfits.

In the courtyard of the Ducal palace I drew a Pierrot curtsying to the fear-some figure of a medieval physician, who wore the bird-mask these doctors donned during plague epidemics, and a just as medieval sorceress lugubriously bedecked with all the evil insignia, charms and counter-charms of a night-hag's magic.

As it got closer to Ash Wednesday – when it was all to end with a great Ballo in Maschera – this enormous mass of euphoric people had begun to present improvised theater and ballet. Every campo, bridge and vaporetto stop became a stage. In the charming cul-de-sac of the Campo Pisano a brilliant Commedia dell'Arte was improvised. Plumed knights on prancing emblazoned cardboard horses held a heroically bloody joust that was crudely interrupted by a twentieth-century television crew, wielding a huge camera consisting of a wooden box with a tin can as a lens, shooting the tournament, while assistants with long stemmed microphones made of broomsticks with sponges attached at one end, ran around interviewing knights, horses and spectators. Folk dancers in odd pink masks on which black half-masks were painted danced on their wooden clogs with such unbridled peasantish vitality that they infected the whole city.

At midnight a gondola drifted down the Grand Canal on which an enormous paper moon, lit from within, had been mounted, its occupants a masked trio of flute, bassoon and mandolin playing a Vivaldi Concerto.

By 1982 the classical Venetian mask had returned in force. Craftsmen all over town were turning out these lugubrious false faces with the parrot beak nose curved over a jutting lower jaw, as well as hideous hybrids, mixtures of classical Venetian, Disney and comic strip features. Eighteenth-century costumes straight out of Guardi and Longhi were for sale everywhere in shops that sprung up all

over the city. Aspiring marchesi, conti and doges stood trying on pig-
tail wigs, purple silk redingotes, mauve knickers. Girls in jeans in
front of mirrors experimented with tricorn hats, astonished at their
sudden seductiveness.

At the Campo San Vio clarions blared through the thin win-
ter air. A massive doge climbed out of his golden gondola in flowing
scarlet robes and skull cap. Hand in hand with his hoop-skirted
dogessa he climbed on the improvised platform where he was wel-
comed by a politician in a loud sport jacket and horn-rimmed glasses,
reading a much too long speech into a microphone. Trumpeters and
drummers in vaguely medieval accoutrements, frustrated by a too
long inactivity, stood trampling, signaling their impatience with
demonstrative yawns. The doge pulled up his wide sleeve, studied his
wristwatch. The dogessa stamped her foot, shook her curls. Then the
drummers took the initiative, beat a forceful ruffle, immediately sec-
onded by the trumpeters. The speaker looked up from his typescript,
took off his glasses and bowed in resignation. The doge, all smiles
again, led his consort with paunchy grace to his gilded state gondola.
Strapping gondolieri in little skirts of pink satin over white pantyhose
and pink toques with tassels on their man-size heads helped the noble
couple aboard with elephantine gentility. Trumpets sounded, drums
rolled and the gondola floated away.

We were to meet again soon. When we reached the Ponte di

Pugni at San Barnaba, the doge stood on the bridge in courtly conversation with an equally aristocratic figure in black velvet robe and purple beret, Nicoletto, leader of the people of the Campo Santa Margharita. For the supposed doge proved to be no other than Castellani, commander of the forces of the Sestiere di Castello, and this was the solemn moment at which after centuries of bloody conflict the arch-enemies, fellow Venetians after all, celebrated their reconciliation, and swore eternal friendship. Demure virgins offered a cup of wine to both great leaders, who then strode hand in hand to the Campo Santa Margharita behind the trumpeters who, sick and tired of blowing fanfares, preceded them blaring a Souza march with remarkable gusto.

On the campo the choir of the gondolieri was gathering for its Carnevale concert. The men were standing around in their white tunics and wide brimmed boaters, chatting with their retinues of parents, grandparents, wives and offspring, while waiting for still missing tenors and baritones. On the ad hoc platform a trio of accordion, clarinet and guitar was playing the Blue Danube. Young gondoliers and their sweethearts used the respite to waltz a turn or two. Then the choir started to sing its Venetian and Neapolitan folksongs, ballads and sea ditties, sentimental love songs and serenades, sang them con brio, as they should be sung, with the ample tremolos women respond to with contented smiles and warm, good feelings in their bellies. They sang so naturally, so musically, with such warmth that the campo, its old houses, the generations of people who had been born, grew up, loved, begot and died here, seemed to join in the rough bel canto, that for a moment made one believe that perhaps the world had not yet gone raving mad,

that the good life was still possible on earth, literally for a song.

On the Fondamenta della Senza a man and a woman were lifting their spastic daughter out of her wheelchair. She was about twelve. Her little face had been gaily made up in white and sky-blue grease paint. In her harlequin's costume of yellow and white lozenges they walked her along the deserted quay, holding her gently, firmly, so that the three moved as in a disjointed choreography, laughing and joking, the girl crowing with delight. Heartbreaking it was, this heroic pageant of tenderness and courage.

The man on the Campo di Moro – Carnevale or not – sat grinding a large butcher knife on a bicycle converted into a sharpening device. He sat there on his triumph of homegrown technology, pedaling his grindstone, honing and bur-nishing, testing the knife on his fingernail, committed to his craft, in the full digni-ty of his professional skill.

When the dusk had deepened into night, the Campo San Polo was already black with people. The music was not less deafening than that of the Piazza, but it was bearable, for it switched from rock to jazz to waltz. A bridgelike platform had been built for this Ballo macabre on which the searchlights played, throwing islands of soft green, white and gold light on the frenzied mass of dancers in masks, wigs, burnous, hoopskirts and jeans, who jumped across the bridge and filled the great black square. Clouds of smoke were made to rise out of this caul-dron of lustful exhilaration, this bobbing, swaying sea of human bodies. Large white banners on which a crowned face was painted, half-alive, half-skull, as in a perverse mockery of death, had been stretched over this orgy of white and gold

masked figures, of peacock feathers and gold wings, of long red stocking legs and the black velvet capes, those tabarros that excite and stimulate the erotic imagination, transcend it until not a creature of flesh and blood seems hidden in the vast black cloak, not one that can feel hungry, sick, weak, but a promise and incarnation of highest bliss, eternal ecstasy. Behind the dead-white masks hot eyes are mocking, tempting, provoking, bewitching....

I stood there drawing in the dark, letting my eye and hand join in the dance, feeling no cold, forgetting even to check whether my pencil was still marking lines on the paper. Then, suddenly I found myself in a tiny bar, drinking a glass of sour red wine next to a man in a trench coat with a fearful lion's head on his shoulders, which he had to lift for every swig of Campari. He stood hand in hand with an archangel with orange wings attached to her blue sweater of which the zipper was undone. On my left a tall, thin Death had his bony hand around the waist of the Maiden in tutu, with pink pantyhose over ample thighs. The scythe leaned against the bar; a knight in armor slipped away with it, unnoticed. The music of the Ballo was mute here, all one heard was life's noise.

Another Ballo, according to the posters, was scheduled in the Via Garibaldi. But the wide street, once a canal, was dark and empty. Two old men were sitting astride chairs they had for some reason dragged almost to the middle of the grim, dark street to argue angrily, shouting terrible insults at each other. The Ballo must have been cancelled when the population of the Via Garibaldi had evacuated to livelier quarters.

On the long way back to the Piazza along the lagoon, the large towboats

lay silhouetted against the purplish black sky. Masked couples were dallying on the benches. The music from the Piazza came closer and closer when, all of a sudden the streetlights went out, the loudspeakers fell silent. Only far away, from San Giorgio, a few lights were shining across the water. Candles started to appear in windows. One of the towboats switched on searchlights, and let them play over the quay and the darkened houses. For a second they lit a white witch's face under a conical hat, then brushed a bridge, quickly caressing Vittorio Emmanuele's equestrian head, and hit my eyes, blinding me just as I bumped into a buxom Hiawatha in feather headdress. It was not frightening, this blackout, in a city in which one forgets to be afraid of one's fellow humans: The worst to expect is to be pickpocketed, short-changed a few thousand lire.

I had barely reached the Piazzetta when, all of a sudden, the floodlights went on again, the electronic din exploded into this sea of faces under wigs and grease paint, making eyes blink helplessly or stare wide open as in panic. It took a moment or two for the tidal wave of surging, throbbing, crashing decibels to flood the Piazza's bloodstream with the adrenaline that propelled it into a frenzy of twitching arms, jerking legs and buttocks, male and female torsos in spasmodic mobility.

Acrobatic bishops in miters, nuns, harlequins in every color and size were Saint Vitus-dancing in frenzied trances through the barbaric blast of din that reverberated through the Piazza that Napoleon once called "the most elegant drawing room of Europe."

An obese fellow in a Carmelite nun's habit danced a solo farandole, waving a fat missal; an elderly runt in a dirty raincoat with Hotel Ambassador in gold letters on his peaked cap did a complex pas de deux with an asparagus-thin youth in white tie, tails and top hat. I bumped into an old man with a strawberry nose under his tricorn, but dressed in a business suit, who dragged a voluptuous fairy queen with almost bare breasts in unsteady waltzing circles. A veiled nun in black, a scarlet cardinal and an officer of the Guards in a vermilion and gold gala uniform executed tangos of extravagant triangular carnality.

Under the arcade of the Procuratio Nuovo a woman in her seventies lifted her skirts high under her short fur coat and started to waltz a solo on old, thin legs. She waltzed and waltzed, until she became twenty again. Her husband, puffing his pipe with a worried frown, stood watching her anxiously. A circle formed around the old dancer, their faces a mixture of mockery, astonishment and awe at this reckless waltzing. A girl tried to join her in her dance, but the old woman in her trance did not even notice her, waltzed her long life all over again in suicidal ecstasy, until, all at once the music stopped dead. The lights stayed on this time and after a few moments, inconceivably, miraculously, Vivaldi's Estra Armonico came over the sound system, echoed against the ancient arcades, and made the jerking, quavering mass congeal in bafflement. Was it a mistake? Had someone slipped this record into the stack to show that Venice had not completely betrayed and forgotten its heritage, nor her preto rosso, Vivaldi, that greatest of magicians, who could let all the birds of all seven heavens sing his exultant joy? Two girls in classical Venetian costume were the only ones that danced, moved lithely, gracefully, in this multitude that stood as if unnerved by the too sudden withdrawal of its auditory drug.

I fled as fast as I could into the Merceria, afraid of the moment the spell would be broken, the rock noise would explode again, taking Vivaldi with me, so that when I reached the Ponte di Frari, the brightly lit rose window of the great church of Santa Maria Gloriosa di Frari stood reflected in the black canal, a gigantic multi-colored moon.

A stone's throw from home, where in his little shrine under the sottoportego, Saint Anthony of Padua tenderly holds the Bambino on his arm among plastic Sweet Williams and roses, a stout man in white clown's garb stood arguing with the saint. He had his black half-mask pushed back on his forehead. His face was that of a sexagenarian who ate too much. He knocked on Saint Anthony's window, so that the electric red votive light flickered, addressing the saint not quite discourteously, but man to man, forcefully.

"Ecco!" he said, "why don't you do something at last? You think I enjoy coming here to bother you night after night? Eh? Eh? Bah!"

He made chopping motions with his right hand, his left hand was stretched out behind his back. But then he froze, raised his chin, crossed himself, and stalked away. Unsteadily he turned the corner and stopped to contemplate the water of the Rio Marin, almost immobile, blue-black, with a Vermeer-like pointille of highlights.

22 ❧ *The Islands*

It was on a fresh sunny winter afternoon that for the first time I took the vaporetto on the Fondamenta Nuove, crowded with people from Mazzorbo and Burano who come to Venice to work and shop. After two short stops at Murano the boat glided across the oil-smooth lagoon that is tideless here, past deserted islets with ruins of chapels and convents. Then it veered into a narrow canal, almost a Dutch canal, with some tumbledown fisherman's cottages on its left bank, and stopped at Mazzorbo, a melancholy island with dark brick houses huddled together like invalids, connected by a wooden footbridge with Burano where the vaporetto stops once more before its endpoint, Torcello.

Burano is colorful, with all the charms of the routine picturesque for the standardized tourist with his camera: little pastel colored houses, toy bridges over toy canals, lacemakers, fishing boats with old salts repairing nets, even a famous restaurant. To me Burano smells of inbred dullness, induces an instant claustrophobic flight to its edges, where limitless spaces open up, on the one side toward the vast sea marshes of Torcello, on the other side past the leaning Campanile the endless sky over the beige mud flats with San Francesco del Deserto, on the horizon Mazzorbo's tower, known as the Lantern of the Dead....

Torcello, just a few minutes away, rises, a high sandbank with wetlands hardly breaking the surface of the sleeping, tideless lagoon. Its name, originally Turicellum, was given to it by the fugitives from Altinum whose bishop during the Barbarian invasions of the fifth century had seen it in a vision as the refuge where his flock would find shelter and safety. It was settled between the fifth and seventh century, eventually became a rich town, long before Venice, seven miles to the south, even existed. Torcello had its dockyards, a thriving wool industry, monasteries and a fleet that traded all over the Levant. In the tenth century Torcello's population had grown to thirty thousand. It has dwindled to less than a hundred today, for when the tides withdrew from this part of the lagoon, its harbors became sanded into a malarious lake. Not a trace is left of the prosperous medieval city: Torcello reverted almost to the state in which the refugees from Altinum found it a millennium and a half ago.

Seen from the landing stage of Burano the tall, austere tower of the cathedral of Santa Maria Asunta shoots up from the wild vast stretches of swampy meadowland. At the landing the vaporetto turns around in a vast sweep for the return trip to the Fondamenta Nuove. Here the world has ended, history's nightmare is finished forever. Torcello's karma is burned out.

> *What it is that dwelleth here*
> *I know not,*
> *yet my heart is full of awe*
> *and the tears trickle down.*

This little Japanese poem written in the eleventh century, at the time of Torcello's ordeal, and at the other side of the globe, epitomizes what I feel each time I set foot on this islet, each time it comes to mind.

I know not, either what it could look like in summer choked

with tourists, music blaring perhaps from the Locanda Cipriani, once a simple country inn, which under the management of Harry's Bar – that second Venetian "must" for the pecunious, sophisticated tourist, almost the rival of the San Marco – has become a mundane, expensive restaurant.

I only love wintry Torcello, flee to it when saturated with the crowds of souvenir hunters in the Merceria. I find its silence to refresh, re-charge, rejuvenate me with unsuspected freshened perceptions.

Wandering over the moors, I found my old legs jumping effort-lessly across deep gulleys, as I tried to stalk two white herons that played hide and seek with me, teasingly landing across ditches, letting me come close, taking off again with a lazy unfolding of wings over bushes of forsythia.

In a garden run wild under tangled arbors, sculptures of noseless admirals, long dead, armless, aimless goddesses, headless saints, line a path that runs all the way to the lagoon. At the water's edge a dozen ducks are diving and dallying in the luminous emptiness as in a Sung painting.

I know of no other place on earth more intensely suffused with the numinous than Torcello in winter. Vézelay has such sanctity, but it still bears the imprints of cruel, tortured turbulence, which here are stilled and exorcized. On Torcello it is each time as if I entered a realm that had transcended the everyday world of death and suffering. Its light is intense, yet never blinding: the darkness of history is overcome, the natural has been distilled into a sublimity that is supernatural, as if the radiance on the meadows were filtered through a medium more diaphanous than air.

If Torcello is haunted its phantoms are nirvanic, angelic, in Piero della Francesca's and Fra Angelico's powder blue and gold.

I mentioned Mazzorbo and hesitated. Mazzorbo, with its Lantern of the Dead, is said to be haunted....

Close to the footbridge to Burano stands a lone dilapidated chapel, flanked by the tall fourteenth-century tower in an empty field, a churchyard where not a tombstone is left. Between a few balding cypresses stand some benches, a swing and a rusted iron see-saw thrown down on the coarse, pockmarked grass. I did not see a single ghost. I just was aware of a presence that did not define itself but sent shivers down my spine, made me jump up and, almost running, cross the footbridge to Burano.

Vast marshy stretches of soft grass and high weeds undulate there over riddlesome mounds and gulleys under the pale blue sky. The endless lagoon, gossamer and motionless, stretches to no horizon, at most to the purplish haze of mountains that rise up from the water at a limitless distance.

It is a landscape that converts itself at once into an inner land-scape, a landscape on the Other Shore, a music of silence as in the

Misericordia of Bach's Magnificat: beyond all sadness and joy, encompassing both. As in Meister Eckhart, God's eye and this human eye are not-two.

Torcello's Cathedral stands with the Palazzo Publicco, now a museum, and the church of Santa Fosca at the dead end of the island's last canal, spanned by the ancient Ponte del Diavolo that leads from the footpath to nowhere but a tangle of vines. The cathedral was built in the seventh century and in the eleventh underwent its last modification. The tall square tower is gaunt and austere, without any ornamentation, as if all conspicuous ostentation was taboo for these refugees who knew the greed of pirates and invaders and of the danger of flaunting one's riches. A row of eighteen columns – time has made them settle in the rhythm of a stilled pavane – leads to a stone altar and connects two mosaics of overwhelming grandeur, that of the Universal Judgement, with God the Father surrounded by the Blessed and by high Byzantine angels, gravely surveys the wicked being cast into hell, devoured by enormous worms, by snakes crawling out of empty sockets. But opposite this Judgement, behind the altar, against her gold mosaic background, stands the Virgin tender yet severe Kami of Torcello, hands raised in blessing over saints and sinners alike, tears of compassion in those grave Byzantine eyes that forever must watch the Judgment across the empty nave.

In the little octagonal church of Santa Fosca that stands in the cathedral's shadow, with its portico of Greek marble and delicately carved capitols, the effigy of the saint rests, frail, blonde and rose in her glass sepulchre suspended in the pink glow of this winter afternoon.

In the absolute silence of dusk the sky becomes old ivory, with faint washes of crimson. The marshes across the wide channel are hidden in a translucent veil of mauve mist. Slowly the sky turns deep indigo. Suddenly the silent shooting star of a jet cleaves it. The oars of a rowboat splash near the far shore, the boat and the man in it almost shadows. A woman's voice rises from the dark marsh. From the emptiness, the vaporetto's yellow light looms up – it passes the jetty, describes its noiseless curve, comes to a halt. The seven minutes to Burano last for a blessed eternity.

At the stop two young nuns herd their class of little boys and girls aboard. In the dim light of the cabin they sit singing a carol, then a Maria hymn: a baroque angel choir brought up to date in yellow plastic raincoats and large blue sneakers.

Already two years have passed since that dusk on Torcello. More than seven hundred times a new dawn has risen; only a few times I have been awake to celebrate the new day; as many times I have missed the darkness falling. Again I am in Venice. The water is still lapping against the old stones of the Fondamente Nuove, the newspaper vendor at the Ponte della Stazione greets me as if I had never left, remembers it is "Le Monde" I want...Signor Mario still stands behind

his desk smiling: "With pleasure, Sir! Ah, Monsieur le Professeur, *quel plaisir de vous revoir! Momento, Signorina, scusi!"*

But Felipe, the busboy, is in the army now and Angelina, the blond woman of the pasticeria, had a breast removed. The dark-eyed little daughter of the cobbler on the Rio Marin, Gina, has become a woman, that is obvious, quite a little woman.

Astonishing! The heart of the Speaker of the Grand Council of the Campo Santa Margharita — has stopped in the midst of an all too passionate denunciation. He moved to San Michele. Still the gondolas, bunched together, float through the velvet evening down the Grand Canal. I recognize Giacomo, the accordionist with his lopsided face, but there is a new, young baritone, who bellows the "O, Sole Mio."

But Gina's babies will grow up in a highrise of Torino. On the scaly green door on the left at the entrance of the Ghetto, a sign announces: "The Shammes does not live here anymore." Whatever that

may mean, such a sign should hang at Venice's entrance: nobody lives here anymore!

This may well be exaggerated, although on my last visit the cosy little grocery where I bought my gorgonzola mascapone is closed. The tailor who repaired the tear in my raincoat is gone. There are only a few children playing on the campi. Old men and women on canes shuffle among the crowds of tourists, who push them aside on the bridges. But the stage set is splendid as ever; the actors, the porter at my hotel, the impolite waiter at the Pizzeria, who overcharges every tourist, leave after hours for Mestre or Marghera. Venice has become ever more a de-humanized tourist trap.

The lagoon, its craft, its veils, its luminous mists, the silhouette of the Serenissima in the distance are still glorious, incomparable. I feel tears running down my cheeks.

No, it is not finished, it is not finished. God is still blowing His soap bubbles....

Typesetting: Graphic Communications and Product Design Inc./NYC

Set in Adobe Garamond with swash italic. Type design by the great

French Designer Claude Garamond in c.1540.

Paperback first edition of 2000 copies.

Written and drawn by Frederick Franck

Editorial assistance by Claske Berndes Franck and Frances Louise Jennick

Design by Martin Moskof

Printing by McNaughton-Gunn, USA